Allan PINKERTON

Allan PINKERTON
The Original Private Eye

Judith Pinkerton Josephson

 Lerner Publications Company • Minneapolis

For their critique of the manuscript and encouragement, my gratitude to Edith Fine, Karen Coombs, Jill Hansen, Catherine Koemptgen, Mary Pinkerton, and to my Encinitas writers' group. Thanks to fellow writer and Scotsman Jerry McStravick, who gave me the Gorbals details I needed. Crucial to my research were Pinkerton, Inc., as well as the Chicago Historical Society, the Huntington Museum, the Library of Congress, the Carlsbad Public Library, and the San Diego State University library. Thanks also to Margaret Brown, for making it possible for me to visit Pinkerton's Security & Investigation Services. For permissions granted, G. P. Putnam's HarperCollins Publishers, and Indiana University Press.

Thanks to my editor, Martha Brennecke, for shepherding the manuscript through its various stages, and for continuing to ask the right questions. Also, thanks to my husband, Ron, and daughters, Kirsten and Erika, for their patience and support.

Library of Congress Cataloging-in-Publication Data

Josephson, Judith Pinkerton.
    Allan Pinkerton : the original private eye / Judith P. Josephson.
        p.   cm.
    Includes bibliographical references and index.
    Summary: Examines the life of the detective who founded his own agency and introduced a system of recording criminals to help track them down and tie them to crimes.
    ISBN 0-8225-4923-9 (alk. paper)
    1. Pinkerton, Allan, 1819–1884—Juvenile literature.
2. Detectives—United States—Biography—Juvenile literature.
3. Pinkerton's National Detective Agency—History—Juvenile literature. 4. Private Investigators—United States—Biography—Juvenile literature. [1. Pinkerton, Allan, 1819–1884. 2. Detectives 3. Pinkerton's National Detective Agency.]
I. Title.
HV7911.P4675J67   1996
363.2'89'092—dc20
[B]   95-13222

Manufactured in the United States of America
1 2 3 4 5 6 01 – JR – 00 99 98 97 96

For my mother, Mary W. Pinkerton,
who has always believed in me

Contents

A Spy's Worst Nightmare

1865

The spy awoke at dawn, rested from his night's sleep. For days he had traveled through the South, secretly gathering information for the Union army: locations of roads, bridges, and enemy camps, and names of Confederate leaders.

After breakfast he stopped in the barbershop for a much-needed shave. The barber stropped the blade of the open razor on the leather. He slathered shaving cream on the spy's face and, with the gleaming blade, shaped and trimmed the man's bristly beard. Suddenly, the barber paused midstroke.

"Mr. Pinkerton?" the barber said with a thick German accent.

"Wha—? I don't know the man," the spy said, his face like stone. The barber didn't look familiar, but being recognized was a spy's worst nightmare.

The barber frowned. "Remember? I shave you . . . many times . . . at the Sherman House in Chicago?"

The spy leaped from the chair, swiping lather from his face. Angrily, he said he didn't know the barber or Mr. Pinkerton, nor would he want to know "any damned Yankee abolitionist." He stormed from the shop.

Allan Pinkerton is recognized in a barber's shop.

Late that night, the spy slipped quietly out of town. Riding hard, he headed north to his Secret Service headquarters in Cincinnati, Ohio. His report pleased his Union army commander.

The barber had been correct. His customer *was* Allan Pinkerton.

Pinkerton's work as a pioneering private eye touched the lives of many powerful people—some distinguished, like President Abraham Lincoln, others notorious, like outlaw Jesse James.

Pinkerton's National Detective Agency—a private police force—became known as "America's Scotland Yard." Allan Pinkerton, called "The Eye" because of the agency's symbol of a wide-open eye, became one of the most famous detectives who ever lived.

In Glasgow, Scotland, narrow streets called wynds *opened onto* closes, *passageways that led to large courtyards surrounded by apartment buildings. Women washed clothes in these courtyards in primitive washhouses, then hung the clothes outside their apartment windows—or inside when it rained, which it often did.*

Growing Up in the Gorbals

1819–1842

Childhood didn't last long in the grimy slums of Glasgow, Scotland. Like most poor children in the 1820s, Allan Pinkerton had left school by age 10 and had a job.

Each day before dawn, Allan climbed out of bed in the small drafty flat where he lived with his family. He splashed icy water from the washbowl onto his face. Shivering, he struggled into his clothes and gulped down stale bread and black tea. Some days a bitter, cold wind whistled through the chinks in the walls. Outside on narrow Muirhead Street, it was still dark. Cold, dank fog swirled around Allan. Bowing his head against the wind, the sturdy child pulled his cap down and his sweater collar up.

As Allan hurried across the Glasgow Bridge, he saw the murky brown waters of the River Clyde below. Ocean tidewaters and sewage flowed into the Clyde, and it often stank at low tide. On the other side of the bridge was the pattern-making shop where he worked as an apprentice, learning his trade from an expert.

Allan's dreary neighborhood, the Gorbals, had been called the worst slum in all of Europe. A visitor to the area commented, "I did not believe until I visited the wynds [narrow alleys between buildings] of Glasgow, that so large an amount of filth, crime, misery, and disease existed on one spot in any civilized country." The walls of the decaying red sandstone buildings were blackened with soot. Large families crowded into cramped, run-down apartments called tenement flats. Rats and mice crept along narrow hallways and stairways. People shouted their complaints at each other, and everybody heard.

Outside, horse-drawn carts clattered by. Cobblestones on the narrow twisted streets were often slippery with garbage, human waste, or the vomit of drunks. The stench mingled with the smells of mutton stew and boiled cabbage wafting from open windows.

Glasgow's noisy cobblestone streets

The Gorbals also teemed with the activity of workshops, factories, public washhouses (called "steamies"), pawnshops, and saloons. Grocers, bakers, fishmongers, and butchers sold their wares in the many small shops.

Allan's family lived in a three-room flat on the top floor of a ramshackle building at the corner of Muirhead Street and Ruglen Loan. His father, William Pinkerton, a tall, thin man, was strict with his seven children. William had three girls and two boys from his first marriage. After his first wife died, William married Isabelle McQueen. She gave birth to four sons. Only two survived—Robert and his younger brother, Allan, born August 25, 1819.

Allan and the other Pinkerton children squabbled noisily as they ran between the clothes pegged on lines stretched from kitchen to bedroom. His older brothers were rowdy and headstrong. The eldest, James, was always in trouble. Another brother became a soldier briefly. Allan's sisters married and left home when they were teenagers. The house grew a little quieter then.

The Gorbals was a rough neighborhood and a scary place for children like Allan. Visitors passing through the Gorbals usually carried a pistol or club to protect themselves against robbers. Some people even feared being caught by body snatchers, said to lurk in the shadowy doorways. Body snatchers stole corpses from graves and sold them to medical schools for dissection. But a popular rumor said that some body snatchers found it easier to kill their victims than to dig up corpses.

Despite its lack of warmth and safety, the Gorbals was home to young Allan Pinkerton. Allan had been named after his grandfather, a well-known local blacksmith. Workers and neighbors often passed by the smithy's smoke-filled shop.

Allan was born in this house in Glasgow, Scotland.

The steady *clink! clank! clang!* of his hammer on metal added to the neighborhood sounds.

Allan's father worked as a police sergeant and was keeper of the keys at the old Glasgow jail. Most poor people in the Gorbals worked in the trades—as brewers' helpers, hand loomers, spinners, pattern makers, or butchers.

William Pinkerton, a weaver by training, had become a police officer in an attempt to make a better life for his growing family. Police work was steady, unlike the trades, where strikes and layoffs often put people out of their jobs.

But when Allan was only nine, his father was killed during a struggle with a prisoner, and the family sank deeper into poverty. Allan's mother worked at a spinning mill, twisting cotton and wool fibers into long strands of thread and yarn. Still, the money she brought home wasn't enough for the family to live on. So, like many other Gorbals children, Allan left elementary school. He went to work for his father's friend Neil Murphy, a prominent Glasgow pattern maker. The few pennies Allan earned each day as an apprentice helped buy food and coal.

Neil Murphy's patternworks made patterns for cloth and other materials, such as the colorful, detailed shawls created from thread made in Paisley, a city on the west border of Glasgow. The shop was cold and damp. Allan's fingers cramped from working with the intricate tools and equipment. Great Britain's Factory Law limited how many hours children under 12 could work each day. But where Allan lived, people didn't have time to worry about overworked children, who often spent 12 to 14 hours at their jobs. Allan's friend Robbie Fergus worked long hours as a printer's apprentice.

By the time Allan finished work, it was dark again. Lamplighters were just lighting the gas street lamps as he hurried back across the Glasgow bridge toward home.

After his father died, Allan, his mother, and his brother Robert became very close. Allan worried about the long hours his mother spent working, and he waited anxiously for her to come home from the mill each night. When she saw her youngest son standing at the corner of Muirhead Street, her weary face brightened into a smile. Sometimes she brought home an egg, a rare treat.

At age 12, bored with the long, bone-wearying hours in the pattern-making shop, Allan quit his job. He decided to become an apprentice to William McCauley, a Glasgow cooper. Coopers made the wooden tubs, casks, and barrels that people used for storing beef, grains, ale, beer, wine, and other goods.

For six years, Allan worked hard learning the cooper's trade. Then on December 26, 1837, he became an official cooper. In a ceremony at a tavern called O'Neil's Public House, Allan received his journeyman's card. This card meant Allan had completed his apprenticeship and could work as a full-fledged cooper. Armed with his new skill, he could now make his own living.

The Allan Pinkerton who had been a tough and plucky boy was now an ambitious and opinionated young man. The husky cooper stood 5 feet, 10 inches tall and had powerful shoulders and arms from swinging a cooper's adz, an axe-like tool used in making barrels.

Allan became a tramp cooper, traveling from town to town to make barrels and kegs. He kept just enough money to pay for his lodging, food, and supplies. The rest of his earnings he sent home to his mother.

A cooper's tool called an adz was used for shaping wood.

At that time, Britain's wealthy people owned most of the land and factories and controlled the government. When 20-year-old Allan returned to Glasgow in 1838, he heard about a group of social reformers called Chartists. The Chartists, who were working-class people, favored a bill called the People's Charter. The People's Charter would give voting rights to all citizens, not just those who owned property. The charter would also grant all citizens a secret ballot, annual elections, equal voting districts, and the right to join the Parliament—Britain's lawmaking body.

The Chartists wanted everyone to have a nice home, good clothing, and plenty of food and drink. Allan Pinkerton owned only one worn suit and one pair of shoes. What the Chartists said sounded just and fair to him.

In the spring of 1839, Allan represented his coopers' union at the Chartist convention in Birmingham, England. People noticed the dark-haired young man with the direct blue-gray eyes. He was known as a serious, quiet, hardworking barrelmaker. But when he spoke about something he believed in, such as righting a social wrong, he became intense, his words fiery and explosive.

When the British government refused the Chartists' demands, leaders of the group couldn't agree on what they should do next. Some Chartists favored using peaceful ways to get what they wanted. Others, like Allan, thought physical force was the best way. The Chartists' motto was "Peaceably if We May, Forcibly if We Must." If necessary, Allan was eager to use his fists and his boots.

Allan and his friends often went to Chartist meetings on the moors—open land overgrown with peat moss and shrubs. The meetings took place at night, probably so that secret plans and defiant words wouldn't be overheard. With torches held high, the Chartists listened to spirited speakers like Feargus O'Conner, a main leader of the movement. Those who favored physical force were planning a march for November 3, 1839. Several groups of Chartists were to gather at Risca, in the nearby country of Wales, then march to Newport. There they would storm Monmouth Prison to free jailed Chartist leader Henry Vincent.

The Glasgow Chartists traveled over 300 miles through rough mountains, freezing rain, and fog to reach Wales. Most of the several thousand marchers who gathered at Risca were poor workers from Great Britain's mills and factories. They were dressed in tattered clothing, with blankets drawn around their shoulders against the cold. Their weapons were their simple tools—axes, picks, iron bars, hammers, sledges, and some old muskets. During the night of November 3, Pinkerton and the other marchers set out in the pouring rain to walk the six miles from Risca to Newport. As they marched, they sang the Chartists' rallying song.

They reached Newport near dawn, but word of the march had spread. British soldiers waited behind closed shutters, their muskets cocked and ready. As soon as the marchers entered the town square, the soldiers opened fire. The Chartists' picks and axes were no match for the British soldiers' bayonets and bullets. In the bloody fight that followed, several of the marchers were injured or killed. Feeling defeated and humiliated, Allan and the Glasgow group began the long trip home, slinking along country lanes and back alleys. The march had failed to rescue the Chartists' jailed leader—but they didn't give up. Allan became more and more involved in the Chartist movement.

Other demonstrations and confrontations followed the march on Monmouth Prison. Often British soldiers attacked

A Chartist meeting, late at night on one of Scotland's moors

the Chartists. Sometimes Chartists were killed or arrested. Allan later said, "I wasn't on the side of the law then. We were all Chartists. . . . Wherever we showed our heads, the police clubbed us."

Several months after the march on Monmouth Prison, Glasgow spinners—Allan's mother among them—went on strike for better working conditions. To help the spinners raise money, Allan asked a group of singers from the Center Street Unitarian Church to give a concert. Allan's coopers' union helped sell tickets.

On the night of the concert, O'Neil's Public House overflowed with people. Some had to sit on benches outside. Allan, wearing polished boots and his only suit, sat with his mother in the front row. The crowd clapped as the performers sang the Scottish songs everybody loved.

A slender young woman with rosy cheeks, dark hair, and fair skin began singing in a clear contralto voice. Allan couldn't help staring at her. He thought she was the best singer in the room and the prettiest girl he'd ever seen. The crowd loved her and stamped their feet when she took a risk by ending the evening with a rousing version of the Chartist song. The government had banned the singing of that song in public.

Allan wanted to know who the singer was. He asked his boyhood friend and fellow Chartist Robbie Fergus, who said the singer's name was Joan Carfrae. She worked as a bookbinder's apprentice in nearby Paisley.

From that night on, Allan couldn't stop thinking about the lovely young woman. Her singing group gave other concerts in support of various unions. Allan went to all the concerts, got to know her, and often walked Joan home. In Allan's words, he started "hangin' around her an' sort of clingin' to her. . . . I had my eyes set on one wee lass. . . . I knew I couldn't live without her." Joan, 18, felt the same way about Allan.

But Allan's involvement with the Chartists soon got him into trouble. The government had published a list of Chartists with Allan's name on it. Before long, the authorities were hunting the Glasgow streets for Allan.

Some of Allan's fellow Chartists were already in jail. Others had fled to America, attracted by the spirit of freedom and tolerance there. Allan's friend Robbie Fergus had settled in Chicago, Illinois, along with many other Scots. For several months, Allan hid in friends' homes. For the first time in his life, he felt like an outlaw with a price on his head.

When Joan heard that the police were after Allan, she hurried to the coopers' union. She talked Allan's friends into leading her to Allan's hiding place.

Allan gave Joan upsetting news. He told her he was thinking about going to America, and not just because he feared for his life. Exciting things were happening in that country. He'd read letters from Scots who'd gone there. They said America was much better than Scotland for working people. Allan hated to give up fighting for the Chartist cause, but he longed for the chance to be truly free and to escape the Gorbals slum. Allan later wrote, "In my native country I was free in name, but a slave in fact. I toiled in and out of season, and my labor went to sustain the Government."

Joan's heart sank at Allan's news. She didn't want Allan to be arrested. She didn't want him to leave either.

Then Allan said, "'t would be a pretty lonesome business without my bonnie singin' bird 'round the shop." He asked Joan to go with him.

Joan's answer was to sing Allan a simple Scottish love song. From the words she sang, Allan knew that "she'd go, too, and God bless her, she did!"

This rare photo of Allan and Joan Pinkerton was taken in the 1870s.

"A Little Job in the Detective Line"

1842–1847

O n March 13, 1842, Allan Pinkerton and Joan Carfrae were secretly married. Allan was 22, Joan just 20. A few weeks later, the two hurriedly said good-bye to their families. Allan promised his mother and Robert that he would send for them as soon as he could.

In the half-light of dawn on April 9, Allan's former employer, pattern maker Neil Murphy, smuggled Allan and Joan aboard the *Kent,* a ship bound for America. To pay their way, Allan would serve as the ship's cooper and sleep in the crew's quarters. Joan would sleep below in steerage, where the cargo was stacked. People who bought the cheapest tickets stayed there.

But when the other passengers learned Joan and Allan had just been married, they convinced the captain that the newlyweds needed to be alone on their "honeymoon." The captain let the young couple have a cabin to themselves.

The Atlantic crossing took four weeks. Howling winds and gigantic waves tossed the ship like a toy boat. Supplies

Poor immigrants to the United States made the ocean crossing inside a ship's steerage.

ran low. Many days Allan and Joan huddled in their cabin, too seasick to move. When the ship neared Canada, huge chunks of late-winter ice trapped the ship and poked holes in the hull. As the ship filled with ice-cold water, frightened passengers jumped into lifeboats and rowed to shore.

The lifeboats landed on sand-swept Sable Island off the coast of Nova Scotia. So many ships had sunk there, it was called the "graveyard of the Atlantic." The island's only inhabitants were Native Americans who immediately searched the band of shipwrecked Scots for jewelry or trinkets. One man demanded that Joan give him her wedding ring. Terrified, Joan refused. But Allan convinced his trembling bride to give her ring to the native. Throughout her life, Joan never wore another wedding ring.

Rescued by another ship, the Pinkertons traveled on to Quebec and then to Montreal on a coastal mail steamer. In Montreal, Allan worked for a few months making barrels to hold beef. Allan and Joan had few belongings and very little money. But here Allan was safe from British soldiers. He and Joan set up housekeeping in their tiny rented room.

Soon Allan had earned enough money for them to go to the United States. But when he told Joan he'd bought steamer tickets, she burst into tears. The ship was to set sail that very afternoon for its journey through the Great Lakes. Joan explained to her baffled husband that she had given a hatmaker a small deposit to hold a "wee bonnet" for her until she could pay him the rest. She begged Allan to exchange the steamer tickets and work a few days longer so she could buy her bonnet.

"I roared like anything, but let her have her way," Allan said later. A few days after the ship departed, newspaper headlines announced that a boiler on the ship had exploded. The ship had sunk with no survivors. From then on, Allan decided his "song singin' wee wife" could have "her way about bonnets."

After traveling by ship and wagon, the Pinkertons landed in Chicago, a fast-growing city of 7,600 people on the edge of Lake Michigan. The air was filled with the pungent odors of people and horses, and with the insistent bellowing of cattle on their way to slaughter. Spring rains and melting snow had turned Chicago's dirt roads into mucky swamps. Wagon wheels sank into the brown, gooey mud. People crossed the streets at the corners, walking across on wooden planks.

A homesick Joan saw a rough place very different from where she had grown up in Duddingston, just outside the lovely, culture-filled city of Edinburgh. But Allan liked Chicago's energy and hustle-bustle. Chicago was what Allan thought America was all about.

Allan and Joan went to stay with his old friend from Scotland, Robbie Fergus, now a Chicago printer. Often other Scottish families gathered at the Fergus home. Joan sang some of their favorite songs—"Annie Laurie," "Loch Lomond," "The

Land of the Liel," and others. Her lovely voice brought back memories of the heather-filled hills of the highlands and the faint echo of Scottish bagpipes. Robbie, Allan, and Joan put together a songbook of Scottish ballads.

With Fergus's help, Allan found a job as a cooper at Lill's Brewery on Chicago's North Side. He rowed across the Chicago River to reach the brewery, where the work was hard and the pay just $.50 a day. Allan yearned to run his own business. He had heard about a pretty little farming town called Dundee, 50 miles north of Chicago. A group of Scots had named the Illinois community after the town of Dundee, Scotland.

In the spring of 1843, Allan headed north alone, telling Joan, "You bide here with Fergus. I'll get a roof o'er our heads first. Then I'll sen' for ye, wife."

Dundee, Illinois, was built on the Fox River.

Joan walked with Allan to the end of Lake Street, then Chicago's western boundary. An old pontoon bridge led out over a mud road and into the prairie. Allan kissed Joan goodbye. Then, tools slung over his shoulders, he disappeared into the tall reeds and grasses.

Joan must have wondered how he'd ever find his way to Dundee. She later told a friend,

> My heart was breakin' quite. . . . I could na bear it when the great grass swallowed him up so quick. But I kenn'd [knew] from the brave whistle I could hear, long after I could na see him any longer, that there'd be a wee home soon for us.

True to his word, Allan rebuilt a long one-story frame building into a house and cooper's shop. Close to the beautiful Fox River, the brown wooden building was surrounded by pleasant gardens and fine old trees.

When he finished the house, Allan returned for Joan and took her with him to Dundee. Pinkerton's Cooperage was on its way, and soon Allan had eight apprentice coopers working in his shop. All day long, hammering and clanking sounds rang from the shop as the coopers shaped barrels and drove their metal hoops into place. Allan's workers, many of them German immigrants, often sang or whistled as they worked.

Joan looked back on the days with Allan in this quiet village and remembered simple, peaceful things:

> In the little shop at Dundee, wi' the blue river purling down the valley, the auld Scotch farmers trundling past with the grist for the mill, or their loads for the market and Allan, with his rat-tat-tat on the barrels whistling and keeping tune with my singing . . . they were the bonniest days the gude fayther e'er gae in a' my life!

From their cabin in Dundee, Joan and Allan could see the Fox River. Barges floated by, hauling grain and lumber to Chicago and Lake Michigan. Farmers led cattle to market over the rough oak bridge covered with hand-carved planks.

The Dundee farmers needed all the barrels, kegs, and casks Allan and his apprentices could make. The work went on from early morning until dusk. Allan's days fell into a routine he would follow the rest of his life. He awoke at 4:30 in the morning and went to bed at 8:30 at night, seven days a week.

The Pinkertons now had a daughter, Isabelle (Belle), born August 4, 1843, and a son, William, born April 7, 1846. Allan named his first two children after his mother and father.

Taking care of the growing family and making meals for Allan's workers meant long hours of housework for Joan. Fortunately, Allan had kept his promise to bring his mother and brother over from Scotland. Robert worked in the cooperage. Isabelle helped Joan with the children. The two women were fond of each other. Having Allan's mother with her made Joan miss Scotland less.

Barrelmaking supplies were expensive, and usually Allan couldn't afford to buy them ready-made. So Allan cut his own hoops and poles and split his own wood into narrow strips. Lumber was scarce on the prairies, but Allan knew about a tiny island upriver with plenty of trees.

One day in 1847, Allan poled a raft up the Fox River to the island. After he'd chopped down the trees he wanted, he sawed and trimmed the logs into usable chunks of lumber. Finished with his work, he discovered coals and ashes from a cooking fire.

Allan wondered who would be making a fire on a deserted island in the middle of a river. For several days, he sneaked back to the island. By day he didn't see any people, but there were clear signs—food scraps, bits of paper—that someone had been there. Allan decided to go back at night. He poled up the river in the dark, watching for shadows of rocks and trees against the dark water. He reached the island, hid his raft, hunkered down into the tall grass, and waited.

Soon he heard the steady creaking and splashing of oars. In the moonlight, Allan could see a boat inching toward the tiny island. He heard men's faint voices. When the boat drew near, shadowy figures crept ashore, made a campfire, and crowded around it.

In the hazy firelight, Allan could barely see, but he heard metal clank on metal. Whatever the men were doing, they were working fast. One man stood watch, peering through the darkness toward the water. Allan didn't move a muscle, even to swat the whining mosquitoes.

Finally Allan slipped away on his raft. The next day, he went straight to Luther Dearborn, the sheriff of Kane County, and told him what he'd seen. Together they watched the island; the nightly visits continued. One night Sheriff Dearborn and Allan Pinkerton led a posse of settlers back to the island and staged a raid on the makeshift camp.

What Allan and the sheriff discovered was a counterfeit gang at work, making fake paper money and coins. The sheriff arrested the men and took their tools and their bags of bogus dimes.

Counterfeit money could be detected by looking for slight imperfections in its printing.

Allan usually received produce, not money, in exchange for the barrels he made. But Allan knew counterfeiters were a big problem on the frontier, and they had swindled many of his customers. At the time, money wasn't printed in official government mints. Banks and other companies printed their own money. People in Dundee trusted only "George Smith money," made by frontier banker George Smith.

Suddenly Allan Pinkerton was a hero. People stopped at his shop to hear how he had caught the "coney men," as Allan called the counterfeiters. From then on, the counterfeiters' island was called "Bogus Island." Allan's reputation grew.

One hot summer day, two well-known Dundee merchants, H. E. Hunt and I. C. Bosworth, asked to see Allan Pinkerton. Shoeless and dressed in overalls and a faded checkered shirt, Allan moseyed down the dirt road to Hunt's general store.

The two shopkeepers got right to the point. They had heard about Bogus Island. They asked Allan if he would be interested in doing "a little job in the detective line."

Allan laughed and said his line of work was being a cooper. Anyway, he wasn't at all sure about getting into such a "will-o'-the-wisp piece of business." Yet Allan was flattered and interested.

Hunt and Bosworth explained that an old codger named Crane, who lived in nearby Libertyville, was suspected of passing counterfeit bills—but nobody had ever been able to prove it. Now a man known as Smooth John Craig was asking for directions to Old Man Crane's place. The Dundee merchants wanted Allan Pinkerton to find out if Craig and Crane were making phony $10 bills.

Allan had heard about Crane. Nearly every swindler and cheat who came to Dundee asked for Old Man Crane. But

Allan had never even seen a $10 bill, a large sum of money then. How could he possibly spot a fake one? Allan studied the real $10 bill the merchants showed him. Then he boldly strode down the street toward Eaton Walker's harness shop, where Craig was having his saddle repaired.

The stranger had a rough-looking face and keen eyes. Allan sized up the man's fancy clothes and his sleek thoroughbred horse. Bulging out of Smooth John Craig's inner coat pockets were the handles of two finely mounted pistols.

Allan struck up a conversation with Craig about his horse, then gave Craig directions to Old Man Crane's. Casually, Allan mentioned that Old Man Crane was a man to depend on, "as good as cheese."

Smooth John looked hard at Allan. Then the two men arranged to talk later that afternoon.

Allan tells Craig the way to Old Man Crane's.

Allan knew he'd have to be careful. Craig might suspect he was laying a trap. Craig had two pistols, while Allan had only his fists to defend himself. But never one to hesitate, Allan went to meet Craig in a grassy ravine outside town.

Craig questioned him. What did he do for a living? How was business? Allan said he was a cooper, but that things weren't going so well and he needed cash. Allan made it sound as if he didn't care if the money was real or fake.

The conversation went well. Still, the two men were wary of each other. But finally Craig said, "I haven't shown you what I've got. . . . Here are my beauties." Craig pulled out two $10 bills. To Allan they didn't look quite the same as the real one he had studied earlier. They weren't. Craig offered to sell Pinkerton 50 fake $10 bills for $125 in hard cash. They'd close the deal at Elgin Academy, a school being built nearby.

Allan walked the five miles back to town, where Bosworth and Hunt gave him the $125. Then Allan hurried to the unfinished basement of the school to meet Craig. After Craig took the cash, he made Allan leave the room. When Allan returned, Craig was gone. The bogus bills lay under a rock.

Allan knew that the sheriff had to catch Craig with the counterfeit money in order to arrest him. So Allan arranged to buy a larger number of bills from Craig in Chicago. At that meeting, Allan and a Chicago deputy sheriff arrested Craig while he still held the counterfeit bills.

At the court hearing, Allan told the jury exactly what had happened. The jury found Craig guilty of passing counterfeit money. The judge slapped Craig into jail.

Back in Dundee, the two shopkeepers urged Allan to ask banker George Smith for money. They thought Allan could be reimbursed for his Chicago expenses. After all, it was Smith's $10 bills that Craig had been counterfeiting.

When Allan meets Craig in Chicago, the counterfeiter is caught.

For this meeting, Joan pressed Allan's best shirt and pants and polished his boots. Dressed for the big city, Allan told his story to the banker behind the large shiny desk.

Mr. Smith, a fellow Scotsman, listened. Then Smith angrily shook his finger at Allan and in a thick brogue said, "Ye was not authorized tae do this wark and ye have nae right t' a cent. I'll pay this, I'll pay this; but mind ye noo . . . if ye ever do wark for me ag'in that ye have nae authorization for, ye'll get ne'er a penny, ne'er a penny."

Embarrassed, Allan took his money and left. Never again would he tackle a job without first agreeing upon the terms. But Allan Pinkerton had successfully completed his first detective job.

Allan Pinkerton

A Detective Agency Is Born
1848–1853

In quiet towns like Dundee, the arrest of a counterfeiter like Smooth John Craig was big news. Impressed with Pinkerton's determination, Sheriff Dearborn asked Pinkerton to act as a part-time deputy sheriff.

Allan still worked long hours in the cooperage. But whenever Sheriff Dearborn needed help, Allan set his cooper's tools aside, put on his badge, and took off after a horse thief, bank robber, or counterfeiter.

During this same period in time, a heated debate over slavery divided the United States. Most people in Southern states depended on black slaves to farm their plantations. People in the industrial Northern states, like Illinois, did not own slaves. From early boyhood, Allan Pinkerton had valued liberty and free institutions. He thought people should not be able to buy and sell other human beings like furniture or cattle. Pinkerton became an abolitionist, someone who wanted to end slavery.

Soon the Underground Railroad stopped at Pinkerton's Dundee cooperage. This "railroad" had no tracks or trains. It was a secret network of "safe houses," where abolitionists gave runaway slaves food and shelter. Many of the "conductors," those who led the groups north, were former slaves themselves, like the famous escaped slave Harriet Tubman. Late at night, the Pinkertons would hear a soft knock on the door. At the exchange of a whispered password, they swiftly whisked the runaway slaves inside. These desperate, frightened fugitives had traveled for days, hunted like animals.

Joan fed the slaves a warm meal. Then the Pinkertons helped speed them toward safe houses in Chicago where the runaways boarded ships and continued their journey northward. Over the next several years, the Pinkertons helped many runaway slaves escape.

In 1848 Allan Pinkerton ran as a candidate for the antislavery Liberty Party. He lost the election, probably because older town leaders thought Pinkerton's views on slavery and other issues were too liberal.

Allan grew tired of small-town life in Dundee, where everyone meddled in everyone else's business. When the chance came for him to become a deputy sheriff in Cook County in Chicago, he accepted the offer gladly. He sold the cooperage, packed up his family and belongings in a big wagon, and headed for Chicago.

Both Allan and Joan were proud of their comfortable new home, a white two-story frame building on Adams Street. Colorful flower gardens surrounded the spacious house. The Pinkertons needed the room, as their family now included twins Robert and Joan, born in December 1848. With hired help more available in the city, life was easier for Joan Pinkerton.

Chicago had grown in the five years that the Pinkertons had been living in Illinois. Tall ships and barges now docked in Chicago's harbors, filled with cargo from grain elevators

A canal completed in 1848 linked Chicago with the Mississippi River system. Transportation became a major industry, and the city's population boomed.

that lined the shores of blustery Lake Michigan. Railroad tracks fanned out from the city's center like spokes on a wagon wheel. To serve Chicago's 28,000 residents, new houses, hotels, churches, and theaters sprouted as fast as builders could nail boards together. Stockyards and meatpacking plants sprawled across the flatlands stretching west of the city.

Chicago's booming growth also attracted outlaws and criminals, rough characters hoping to profit from the city's growing businesses. But Allan wasn't afraid to use his fists when chasing armed thugs. Almost 30 now, Allan could wrestle an opponent to the floor.

In 1849 Chicago's mayor appointed Pinkerton the city's first private detective. When two Michigan girls were kidnapped, Sheriff William Church asked Pinkerton to find them. He tracked the girls down in Rockford, Illinois, and rescued them, shooting one of their kidnappers.

Allan left this job after just a year. He still wanted to fight crime, but he wanted independence from politicians and the corruption that weakened the city's small police force. Sheriffs could be bought off, Allan knew, and criminals often went free.

Allan Pinkerton saw that there was a clear need for honest people dedicated to law and order. In 1850 he and Chicago attorney Edward A. Rucker started the Northwest Police Agency. The two men opened a small office in downtown Chicago. The agency's motto was "We Never Sleep." A wide-open eye was the company logo. Rucker left the agency after just a year to become a judge, so Pinkerton was on his own. He later renamed his agency Pinkerton's National Detective Agency.

At that time, few detective agencies existed in the United States. Pinkerton decided his agency would catch criminals, recover stolen property, gather information, and investigate fraud. In one of the agency's early cases, Pinkerton caught a famous French check forger who had outwitted New York City police with his fake signatures. Other cases the agency handled involved safecracking and train robberies. Detectives spied on streetcar conductors who pocketed ticket money and checked on the honesty of railroad employees.

At first the agency was small: a secretary, a few clerks, and a small group of detectives. Many of Pinkerton's first agents had never been law officers before. Some had worked as clerks, merchants, or farmers. Others had been jewelers, boot makers, or clock makers. When choosing his employees, Allan felt that honesty was more important than formal training. Natural instincts and good common sense were what made good detectives. Like him, Allan's agents had to be able to read people's faces. One of his first agents was George Bangs, a bright, tough businessman who would become Pinkerton's office manager and lifelong friend.

Allan Pinkerton wanted people to think of detective work as a business, a respected profession. He gave his investigators a special title, calling them "operatives." He called himself the "principal" or "founder" with the code name "A.P." Operatives had to have "clear, honest, comprehensive understanding, force of will, and vigor of body."

Pinkerton later wrote a code of conduct for his operatives, called the *General Principles of Pinkerton's National*

The logo for the Northwest Police Agency—and, later, Pinkerton's National Detective Agency—was the origin of the term "private eye."

Allan's friend and office manager, George Bangs

Detective Agency. The principles set down firm rules: no shadowing of jurors, no cases involving divorce or marriage, no information based on suspicion instead of fact, no unnecessary expenses, no testimony from witnesses who drank.

The agent's goal was to control the mind of the criminal. To play this difficult role, an agent had to have a sharp mind and the ability to measure a person's character. Secrecy and acting skills were also important. If the detective did the job right, sooner or later the criminal would tell someone about his crime.

Allan did have sympathy for the criminals he caught. Once criminals had served their time, he was willing to help them make a new start. With a kindness masked by his stern manner, Pinkerton arranged for ex-convicts to work in banks and brokerage houses, where they helped watch for forgers and embezzlers.

As Allan Pinkerton's reputation grew, however, he made enemies among Chicago's criminals. One night in 1853, as he was walking home, a shot blazed out of the darkness. As Chicago's *Daily Democratic Press* told the story:

> The pistol was of large calibre, heavily loaded and discharged so near that Mr. Pinkerton's coat was put on fire. Two slugs shattered the bone five inches from the wrist and passed along the bone to the elbow where they were cut out by a surgeon together with pieces of his coat.

Allan's habit of tucking one hand behind his back under his coat when he was thinking something over had saved his life. The bullets hit his arm instead of entering his back.

This Virginia business bought and sold slaves. Allan Pinkerton was a well-known leader in the Underground Railroad movement, helping slaves to escape to the North.

"I Detested Slavery"

1854–1859

Allan continued to build his agency and its reputation for fairness and reliability. The Pinkerton Agency used a huge network of letters, reports, and telegrams to communicate. When the agency took part in an arrest, agents helped strip and search the criminals, noting telling details—facial features, scars, moles.

This information was organized into the Rogues' Gallery, a collection of mounted pictures with facts noted on the back:

* a cowboy with "bloodshot eyes" who was "a good cook"
* a bandit who "plays the violin and bass viol . . . likes to see a good horse . . . quiet and rather reserved . . . shy of strangers"
* a bank robber who had a "scar on his left hand, speaks Mex, and lives with a Hooker named Frisco Ann"
* a forger who "spits freely while he talks, works East St. Louis, and is a friend of the Scratch [Charles Becker, the world-famous forger of banknotes]"
* a safe cracker with "a scar the shape of a half moon on the side of his right eye"

For one case, Allan disguised himself as a bricklayer.

Pinkerton taught his detectives how to track a suspect by "shadowing," following without being seen. When they worked undercover, the detectives often wore disguises. Pinkerton's central office looked like the wardrobe room backstage at a theater. Big trunks held hats, boots, suits, and other clothing. On a specific case, a detective might have to act the part of a bartender, a horsecar conductor, a watchmaker, or a gambler.

Naturally decisive and organized, Pinkerton set up a system for handling each case. First, Bangs or Pinkerton briefed the detective on the facts in the case. They then decided on the proper disguise. With a new identity, the detective took off after his target.

Soon Pinkerton opened branch offices in Wisconsin, Michigan, and Indiana. Detectives filed frequent reports with

Pinkerton and received detailed instructions from the central office in Chicago.

From the earliest days of the agency, Allan did not allow agents to collect rewards. Clients agreed ahead of time to pay fees to the agency, at higher-than-average rates. This meant that Pinkerton's major clients were big businesses, government agencies, or wealthy individuals.

During its first few years, Pinkerton's business grew like a fast-sprouting tree. The agency's work for the railroads helped pay for this growth. From 1851 to 1856, the Illinois railroads added nearly 2,000 miles of track. The railroads increasingly became targets for robbers, freight car looters, and safecrackers. By 1854 several railroads were paying the Pinkerton agency $10,000 a year for protection. Agents carried free railroad passes and blank tickets.

Besides chasing their targets by train, stagecoach, and wagon, Allan and his agents often traveled on horseback. They galloped across prairies and into hills toward outlaw hideouts in remote prairie towns.

No one worked harder than Allan. If an agent couldn't handle a case, Allan often took it over himself. He now had almost more detective work than he could handle.

Despite his busy work schedule, Allan kept up with his abolitionist activities. Allan and Joan continued to hide and feed runaway slaves and to keep people and messages moving along the Underground Railroad. Allan was now a well-known leader in the movement.

Back in 1850, Congress had passed the Fugitive Slave Act. Under the terms of this law, slaves who ran away were committing a federal crime and so were the people who helped the runaways. The Pinkertons were breaking the law and risking fines or imprisonment. In his profession, Allan chased lawbreakers; in his personal life, he broke the law to help slaves escape. Allan probably never saw the contradiction in his actions. To him, the slavery issue was a clear case of right versus wrong. "I detested slavery," he once wrote.

One wintry night in 1859, the Pinkertons awoke to furious knocking at their door. Outside stood an older man with a thick gray beard, piercing blue eyes, and a shock of white hair. The man was the abolitionist leader John Brown. He was leading a group of twelve runaway slaves on a 600-mile journey across the American frontier and north to Canada. Allan welcomed the group into his home without question.

Pinkerton admired and trusted Brown. Some of John Brown's earlier raids in Kansas had resulted in robberies and the brutal murder of five pro-slavery settlers. Blindly devoted to abolishing slavery, Pinkerton justified Brown's violent actions as necessary for the cause.

Abolitionist John Brown

In the days following Brown's arrival, Pinkerton raised $500 to help Brown and the slaves traveling with him continue their journey northward. As Allan watched John Brown board the train, Allan told his young son William, "Look well upon that man! He is greater than Napoleon and just as great as George Washington."

Hoping to start a slave uprising, John Brown and his followers later seized a military storehouse in Harpers Ferry, Virginia. Brown was captured and tried for treason. Pinkerton lobbied for Brown's release, but Brown was finally hanged for his crime.

Along with growing fame, the early years in Chicago brought sadness to the Pinkerton family. The Pinkertons' first child, Belle, was often sick and required constant care. Of the 10 children born to Allan and Joan, only 3 lived to adulthood. In 1854, both Allan's mother and a daughter, Mary, aged two, died. In the spring of 1855, Robert's twin, Joan, died at age six.

When another baby girl was born to the Pinkertons that summer, she became the second Joan. A dark-haired beauty like her mother, this Joan was as spirited and independent as her two brothers and her father. The senior Joan Pinkerton ran the household and cared for her growing children with quiet strength and patience, while her busy husband filled almost every waking hour with work.

Acting as a roving troubleshooter, Pinkerton personally handled a post office case in 1855. Postal clerks were stealing money orders and bank drafts out of the mail rooms. As a special agent for the U.S. Post Office Department, Allan's job was to spy on the employees and discover who the thieves were.

Pinkerton posed as a jolly, dim-witted clerk in the Chicago post office. He made friends with a young clerk,

Theodore Dennison. Theodore and his brother Perry—nephews of Chicago's postmaster—were "pilers," workers who sorted the mail into piles for delivery. Crouched behind mounds of mail, Allan spied on Dennison. The clerk felt each envelope to see if there was money tucked inside. If so, he pocketed it. Later, when Pinkerton broke into Dennison's boardinghouse room, he found $4,000 in bills pasted to the backs of pictures hanging on the wall. Dennison confessed and was arrested.

The next year, Pinkerton's agency hired the first female detective. Kate Warne was a young widow of 23 when she came to Pinkerton's office in 1856 to ask for a job. Police work had always been considered too dangerous for women. But the idea of a female spy intrigued Pinkerton.

Pinkerton asked Warne how she thought she could help his young agency. She suggested that women could make useful spies on trains. Or, disguised as companions, female agents might be able to draw secrets from criminals better than men could.

Pinkerton listened carefully. He studied the tall, slender young woman with brown hair. He thought she had an honest face and eyes "filled with fire." She appeared intelligent and graceful and had a self-confident manner.

Pinkerton told Warne to come back the next day for his answer. All night long, he mulled the idea. Then when Warne returned, he hired her.

Throughout the years Allan worked with Kate Warne, he considered her one of his best detectives and a close friend. In 1858, Warne helped Pinkerton crack a $40,000 robbery case. The Adams Express Company, a large eastern transporter of money and goods, had hired Pinkerton and his agents to investigate one of their employees, Nathan

Maroney. The company suspected him of stealing money from its Montgomery, Alabama, office. Railroad official Edward Sanford had pleaded with Pinkerton to send a man "half horse, half alligator." Pinkerton must have thought he was the man for the job, because he led the case himself, along with other agents.

Kate Warne played her role well as a trusted friend to Maroney's wife. Thanks to Warne's tips and those of other agents, most of the stolen money was found in a farmhouse cellar, more than 1,000 miles from where the robbery had taken place.

The success of the Maroney case marked a turning point for the agency. Soon other express companies trusted Pinkerton to protect their cargo. The railroads took notice, too, and Allan's business grew. He also continued to hire female agents. By 1860 Kate Warne headed a small group of agents that Pinkerton called his "female detective department." These women posed as widows, female companions, or wives of criminals to help trap suspects.

By now, people all across America had heard about Allan Pinkerton, nicknamed "The Eye." Newspapers called Allan Pinkerton a "terror to evil doers." The Chicago *Daily Democratic Press* reported: "As a detective, Mr. Pinkerton has no superior, and we doubt if he has any equal in this country."

Abraham Lincoln was a lawyer when this photograph was taken in 1858. Pinkerton met him about this time, when the two men both worked for the Illinois Central Railroad. In 1860 Lincoln was elected president of the United States.

SIX

The Baltimore Plot

1860–1861

Through his work for the Illinois Central Railroad, Pinkerton met George Brinton McClellan, the new vice president for the railroad. McClellan, 30, was a West Point graduate and engineer. Handsome and bright, he knew powerful people. The two men discussed ways that Pinkerton's agency could protect the railroad from thieves. Pinkerton was immediately drawn to McClellan. In some ways, he was everything Pinkerton wanted to be. They became close personal and professional friends.

With McClellan's encouragement, Pinkerton organized the first guard service in 1860. At first just six uniformed Pinkerton operatives helped protect Chicago's packing plants and commercial houses from thieves. This number grew into a corps of security guards called the Merchants Police.

George McClellan introduced the detective to a tall, gangling attorney from Springfield, Illinois. His name was Abraham Lincoln, and like Pinkerton, he worked for the Illinois Central Railroad. From their first meeting, the two men liked each other. Pinkerton enjoyed Lincoln's wry sense of humor and the way he told stories. Lincoln trusted Pinkerton and respected the work he had done for the railroads.

George McClellan

By 1860, when the nation elected Lincoln its 16th president, the United States was on the brink of civil war. Lincoln had spoken out strongly against slavery during his debates with Stephen A. Douglas in 1858. Southerners now threatened to fight for their right to own slaves.

In December 1860, South Carolina seceded, or withdrew, from the Union (the United States). Within the next six months, 10 other Southern states also left the Union. Jefferson Davis became president of these Southern states, known as the Confederate States of America.

On January 19, 1861, about a month before Abraham Lincoln was to go to Washington, D.C., for his first inauguration, Samuel Morse Felton, president of the Philadelphia, Wilmington, and Baltimore Railroad, asked Pinkerton to do some secret work for the railroad. Pinkerton agreed to meet Felton in New York City.

Felton explained that if war broke out, secessionists (Southerners who believed leaving the Union was right) had threatened to blow up bridges and tunnels along the railroad route. They also planned to destroy the ferry boats on the Susquehanna River at the Havre de Grace crossing, cutting off communication between Washington and the rest of the country.

If the North and South went to war, the railroad between New York and Washington was a critical supply link for Northern troops. Maryland was a key middle-ground state, close to the North, but with many slaveholding residents. If Maryland left the Union, the nation's capital might be taken over by the South. Felton wanted Pinkerton to gather information about these dangerous plans.

On January 27, 1861, Pinkerton agreed to go to Baltimore. He warned Felton not to tell anyone, especially politicians, about the mission. Leaving his family behind, Pinkerton, Kate Warne, and Harry N. Davies hurried to Baltimore. Agents Timothy Webster and Hattie Lawton settled in Perrymansville, Maryland, a Confederate post south of the Susquehanna River crossing. Kate Warne wore a coiled black and white ribbon, called a cockade, on her hat. This badge made the secessionists think she was one of them.

Pinkerton and Davies mingled with crowds in restaurants and taverns and listened to fiery speeches at political rallies. People angrily criticized both Lincoln and the Union. Even the police sympathized with the South. Pinkerton heard alarming and persistent rumors about a plot to murder Lincoln before his inauguration.

Pinkerton opened an office on Baltimore's South Street. Calling himself John H. Hutchinson, a financial expert, Pinkerton went out of his way to stop and chat with a Confederate sympathizer named Luckett who had an office down the hall.

Allan normally didn't drink. Or, if he did, it was "just a drop now and then." Yet now he drank and talked with Luckett, and the two men shared ideas and some secrets. Luckett didn't know that "Hutchinson" was just acting a part.

At nearby Barnum's Hotel, Luckett introduced Pinkerton to a hotheaded Italian barber, Cypriano Ferrandini. Ferrandini shouted, "Lincoln shall never be president. . . . I will sell my life for that of the abolitionist. . . . I am ready to die for the rights of the South." Pinkerton pretended to agree with the excitable man.

President-elect Lincoln left Springfield, Illinois, on February 11 in a cold, wintry drizzle. On his 2,000-mile journey, he planned to stop at several cities to share his views with the people. Lincoln faced a huge challenge—to keep the country from going to war over slavery.

In Philadelphia, Lincoln planned to raise a flag over Independence Hall to honor the new state of Kansas. His train would reach Baltimore on February 22. Pinkerton learned that assassins planned to ambush Lincoln as he traveled from one Baltimore train depot to the other.

After talking with Lincoln's trusted friend Norman Buell Judd, Pinkerton arranged to meet with Lincoln at the Continental Hotel in Philadelphia. Railroad president Samuel Felton accompanied Pinkerton, and together they pushed through crowds in the hotel's narrow halls. Bright lights blazed; music played. Excited people milled about, hoping to catch a glimpse of the president-elect.

In a quiet hotel room, Judd repeated Pinkerton's story to Lincoln. Pinkerton watched Lincoln's tired, deeply lined face in the warm light of the gas lamp. Lincoln listened without emotion. Then his gunmetal gray eyes shifted to Pinkerton. Quietly, he asked for more details.

Pinkerton learns of the plot to assassinate President-elect Lincoln.

Pinkerton explained that there were 10 to 15 plotters. They planned to stage a street riot by throwing rotten eggs and broken bricks while Lincoln's open carriage traveled through the Baltimore streets. In the confusion, hidden assassins would attack Lincoln with revolvers and knives, then escape. A steamer lying hidden in a nearby bay would carry the assassins to safety in Virginia. Fiercely behind the Southern cause, the plotters believed that killing Lincoln would make them patriotic heroes and martyrs.

Pinkerton advised Lincoln to cancel all his plans and leave that very night for Washington.

Lincoln said, "No, I cannot consent to this. I shall hoist the flag on Independence Hall tomorrow morning and go to Harrisburg tomorrow." Lincoln didn't want to sneak into Washington. But when further information supported

Lincoln raises the flag over Independence Hall.

Pinkerton's story, Lincoln finally agreed. After his stops in Philadelphia and Harrisburg the next day, he would place his life in Pinkerton's hands.

On February 22, Lincoln raised the flag over Independence Hall and spoke to the legislature in Harrisburg, as planned. Late that night, however, the traveling party gathered in a west Philadelphia train shed just before the train was to leave. Lincoln wore a short bobtailed overcoat thrown loosely over his shoulders and a muffler around his neck. Instead of his usual tall black stovepipe, Lincoln wore a soft wool hat. He looked more like a well-to-do farmer than the future president of the United States.

Accompanying Lincoln was Ward Lamon, a friend and former law partner. Lamon suggested that Lincoln carry a bowie knife and a pistol for protection. This made Pinkerton angry. Even though Lincoln had been a noted frontier fighter,

Pinkerton thought it was ridiculous for the president-elect to enter the capital armed. Besides, it was Pinkerton's job to protect the president. Lincoln smiled and refused the weapon.

The scene at the train station could have been from an action thriller. Steam rose from the giant black locomotive, swirling around the small group in great white clouds and adding to the sense of mystery. The loud puffing of the engine made it hard to hear. Stooping slightly so he'd appear frail and sickly, Lincoln leaned on Pinkerton's arm. Pinkerton nervously smoked a cigar as Kate Warne helped whisk the group on board.

As soon as a messenger told the conductor the presidential party was aboard, the train whistle sounded. Within minutes the train sped through the darkness. Officials had closed off the telegraph lines until Lincoln was safely on his way.

Curtains separated the cold, drafty compartments of the sleeping car. Lincoln had to bend his long legs to fit into the narrow bed. But with the clattering and bumping of the train's iron wheels, he couldn't sleep anyway. Lincoln and Lamon huddled around the wood-burning stove to keep warm. In a soft, low voice, Lincoln spun yarns and told jokes by the dim light of lanterns. Occasionally Pinkerton listened. But for most of the ride, he stood on the rear platform of the train, peering into the frosty darkness, watching closely for lights.

Knowing that plotters planned to dynamite the tracks and blow up the bridges, Allan had posted agents along the route at each bridge siding and crossroad. The agents wore lanterns hanging from their belts. As the train chugged by each post, a guard flashed a white light that signaled "All's Well!" up ahead. The train rolled on and passed quietly through Baltimore at three in the morning. When the train paused briefly at the station, the travelers heard a distant drunk singing

"Dixie," the South's rallying song. The train reached Washington about 6:00 on the morning of February 23.

In creating the getaway scheme, Pinkerton had made up code names. Pinkerton was "Plums," Lincoln was "Nuts." When the train arrived in Washington, Pinkerton sent a message to Lincoln's friend Judd, as well as to other key people. One read:

> Plums arrived here with Nuts this morning—all
> right.

Safe in the capital, Lincoln thanked Pinkerton warmly for his protection and invited him to visit whenever the detective was next in Washington. Lincoln never mentioned how embarrassed he was when the newspapers poked fun at him for having slipped into Washington in disguise.

"Plums" arrives safely with "Nuts" in Washington.

Baltimore was in chaos when Pinkerton returned. People cursed Lincoln and the Yankees, as Northerners were called. Ferrandini and most of the main plotters had disappeared. At the office, Pinkerton ran into Luckett, who swore angrily about the spies who had foiled the plot. Allan listened sympathetically and gave Luckett a $5 donation for the Friends of Southern Rights.

Pinkerton later decided not to charge the railroad for the time spent protecting the president: "I had informed Mr. Lincoln in Philadelphia that I would answer with my life for his safe arrival in Washington, and I had redeemed my pledge."

One month after Abraham Lincoln took office as president of the United States, the country exploded into civil war. On April 12, 1861, the Confederate army fired on Union troops at Fort Sumter in Charleston, South Carolina. The North was at war with the South.

A few days later, Confederate forces blew up the railroad bridges leading into Baltimore and cut telegraph wires to the capital, just as Pinkerton had feared. The Union government scrambled to pull together an army.

On April 21, 1861, Pinkerton sent his best agent, Timothy Webster, to President Lincoln with a secret message. The letter, sewn into the lining of Webster's coat, offered Pinkerton's experienced detective force of nearly 20 people for use as a secret service to the military. Agents could search out traitors and Confederate sympathizers, carry messages, and gather information. President Lincoln sent for Pinkerton.

In Washington, Pinkerton explained his plans for a secret service as Lincoln and his cabinet listened carefully. Overwhelmed with the crisis and still hoping to head off full-scale warfare, they hesitated. Pinkerton waited several days for an answer, but none came. Tired of waiting, he decided to return to Chicago.

On the way home, he stopped in Philadelphia. There, he received word from his good friend George McClellan. The short, scrappy, former railroad vice president was now a Union general and commander of the forces of Ohio, Indiana, and Illinois. General McClellan wanted Pinkerton to form a secret service for this division of the army. Its purpose would be to spy on the South, report enemy activities, and find out how Southerners felt about the war.

Now Pinkerton could put his ideas into action. He set up headquarters in downtown Cincinnati, Ohio. He took with him his most experienced agents—chief assistant George Bangs, Timothy Webster, Kate Warne, Hattie Lawton, Pryce Lewis, John Scully, and others.

Though people might not have recognized Allan Pinkerton, by now they connected his name with the word "detective." So all during the Civil War, Pinkerton called himself Major E. J. Allen. Only Lincoln, McClellan, and Pinkerton's fellow agents knew his real identity.

Traveling alone or in pairs, agents soon fanned out across the border separating the Union from the Confederacy. As Major Allen, Pinkerton also wove back and forth across enemy lines, disguised as a Southern gentleman and riding a beautiful bay horse. Everywhere people talked about the war. Pinkerton talked to important Southern leaders. He asked them questions and listened to their complaints. In secret, he wrote down everything he heard and saw.

When General McClellan wanted someone to measure troop strength in western Virginia, Pinkerton sent his English agent, Pryce Lewis. Pinkerton helped disguise Lewis as a wealthy English lord, complete with clothes of the finest broadcloth, a gleaming top hat, red Russian-leather shoes, and neatly trimmed muttonchop whiskers. After sharing whiskey, port, and cigars with Confederate officers in Kentucky and Tennessee, Pryce Lewis brought detailed reports back to Pinkerton.

In July 1861, President Lincoln appointed McClellan commander of the Army of the Potomac in Washington. McClellan then asked Pinkerton to set up a secret service for the entire Army of the Potomac. Besides observing the enemy, he and his agents were to investigate all deserters, refugees, prisoners of war, and spies. To do so, Pinkerton and his agents relocated to Washington. Timothy Webster and Hattie Lawton moved on to observe rebel activity in Baltimore.

Pinkerton also had to do a job in Washington that he hadn't expected. Word had passed through the War Department that a Major Allen now worked for General McClellan. Soon, a blizzard of paper fell on Pinkerton's desk.

He received complaints about poor army food, ragged uniforms, corrupt local police, and broken-down cavalry horses. Back in Chicago, a dishonest meat packer was butchering cows that looked like skeletons and selling bad meat to the army. Faithfully, Pinkerton tried to deal with each problem. Yet handling endless, trivial details must have been hard for the action-oriented Pinkerton.

But not long after he came to Washington, he received an assignment more to his liking: cracking a spy ring led by a beautiful Washington socialite.

Confederate spy Rose Greenhow in her thirties

The Detective and the Wild Rose

1861–1862

Allan Pinkerton and Rose Greenhow made a striking pair of enemies. The tall, muscular detective was the top lawman in the country. An influential Washington hostess, Rose Greenhow was well educated, clever, and beautiful, with a mane of thick black hair and flashing dark eyes. Allan Pinkerton had lived his childhood in the Glasgow slums. Rose Greenhow had been born into a life of wealth in Maryland.

Rose and her husband, Robert, a prominent doctor, had given many elegant parties in their Washington home. Women in low-cut, lace-trimmed satin and silk dresses with huge, bell-like skirts had swirled gracefully around the dance floor with uniformed naval officers, senators, and other officials.

Rose had been popular with her husband's powerful friends—among them Jefferson Davis, now president of the Confederacy. But since her husband died in 1857, Rose had often been seen with James Buchanan, president of the United States before Lincoln. Known for her sharp memory, dramatic beauty, and graceful manners, Rose fascinated men.

The clash between Rose Greenhow and Allan Pinkerton became a duel of wits and principles. Allan thought slavery was wrong and that Confederates were traitors to their country. Rose believed the South had a right to its chosen way of life. Allan saw the flag of the United States as a symbol of a proud country; Rose now saw the same flag as a symbol of oppression.

Pinkerton and his agents suspected that Rose and other society women were part of a vast spy ring. Rose was thought to report directly to Brigadier General Thomas Jordan of Virginia, who had organized the spy network. Pinkerton's suspicions were correct.

These female spies pretended to care only about entertaining and fun at the lavish parties they gave. But as they flitted among their guests, making polite conversation, Rose and the other women gathered information—from military officers, politicians, and others involved in the war effort. Sometimes Rose and the other women exchanged romantic favors for what they learned. Spies who were clerks, bankers, and Union officers carried the information to Confederate agents.

Jordan hears a report from one of his female spies.

The women used tricks familiar to any 19th century spy. They tucked messages into hollowed-out tobacco plugs, sewed documents into the linings of gowns and men's coats, and stuffed notes into hollow canes. Some women wove secret papers, sewn into silk pouches, into their coiled hairdos.

One of Rose's early successes came in July 1861 in the Battle of Bull Run, one of the first big battles of the Civil War. Rose tipped off the Confederate troops that Union General Irvin McDowell and 55,000 Union troops were headed from Washington toward a showdown at Manassas Junction, Virginia, near Bull Run Creek. Because the Confederates knew about this ahead of time, they soundly defeated the Union soldiers, striking a crushing blow to the Union forces.

Pinkerton agents Pryce Lewis, Sam Bridgeman, and John Scully helped Allan track and shadow Rose in Washington. On a blustery August night, they trailed a young Union officer to Rose's home.

Pinkerton and his agents huddled in the pelting rain. Through the shutters, the dim light from the parlor lamps pierced the darkness. The first-floor windows of Rose's two-story house were too far off the ground for the men to see into the house. So Pinkerton took off his boots and stood on the shoulders of his two fellow agents to peer inside.

The handsome uniformed man and Greenhow were talking in low tones. Pinkerton could catch only bits and pieces of what they said. But he heard enough to understand that the officer was explaining military positions on a map. Furious, Pinkerton wanted to rush into the room and challenge the traitors. Instead he stood silently as rain plastered his clothes to his body.

Next, with a swish of her elaborate silk gown, Rose led the officer upstairs. Pinkerton assumed they were headed for

Pinkerton is captured.

Rose's bedroom. A little while later, the couple returned arm in arm and headed out of the room toward the front door. When the door opened, Pinkerton heard what sounded like a kiss, followed by a whispered good night.

As the officer hurried away from Rose's home, Allan scrambled down from his agents' shoulders. Without stopping to put on his shoes, he crept down the street, shadowing the officer. But the officer realized he was being followed. Once he reached the barracks, he hollered for the military police.

Suddenly Pinkerton found himself surrounded by Union soldiers, their bayonets pointed at his chest. Shoeless, hatless, and covered with mud, Pinkerton looked like a rat fished out of the river.

All Pinkerton would tell his captors was his wartime name, E. J. Allen. He spent the night in a dark, damp jail cell. Still soaking wet, Pinkerton shook with the cold, and his teeth chattered like castanets. He hoped his men had picked up his shoes from under Rose's window.

Finally Pinkerton convinced a kindly guard to slip a message to the assistant secretary of war, Thomas Scott. When Pinkerton was released, he told Scott what he'd observed at Rose's home.

The next day officials searched the living quarters of the young Union officer who had visited Rose. He was arrested, charged with spying, and sent to prison.

Pinkerton now put Rose Greenhow under 24-hour watch. He kept track of when she went out and when she came home. He noted all visitors. Most embarrassing for the War Department, Pinkerton reported the names of key Union officers who visited Rose, describing in great detail what they did in her parlor.

If Rose suspected that Pinkerton and his men were tailing her, she delighted in throwing them off her trail. When she took food baskets to rebel captives, she flounced into Old Capitol Prison to the cheers of the prisoners.

As the days wore on, Washington sweltered in the late summer heat. War fever ran high with talk of battles and casualties. Finally, Assistant Secretary of War Scott decided to put an end to the Greenhow matter. When Rose arrived home one fall day, she was placed under house arrest. As she stood in the street, she calmly swallowed a coded message. Then she swept dramatically inside.

Rose was now captive in her own home, or "Greenhow Prison," as the newspapers called it. Pinkerton and his men scoured her house for evidence.

"Men rushed with frantic haste into my chamber," she said. "My beds, drawers, and wardrobes were all upturned, soiled clothes pounced upon . . . and mercilessly exposed. . . .

Papers that had not seen the light for years were dragged forth . . . every scrap of paper seized." Rose sat with her eight-year-old daughter playing at her feet as the detectives rummaged through her things.

Allan was finding the proof he needed. Reports and other documents he found showed precise locations of Union troops. Pinkerton rescued one letter from the fireplace. He pasted the torn pieces back together and wrote down the names mentioned in the message. In Rose's little red diary, he found lists of her fellow spies and messengers. They, too, were trapped.

The arrests began. Many of the people included prominent citizens—doctors, lawyers, senators, representatives, army officers, and military aides. All were outwardly loyal to the Union, yet their true sympathies lay with the South.

Now Pinkerton and the Union government had to decide what to do with Rose Greenhow. Newspaper stories called her America's most beautiful and dangerous spy. To Confederate sympathizers, she was a brave heroine. Even friends

Pinkerton's most important discovery was the code Rose Greenhow used to communicate with General Thomas Jordan.

who sided with the North felt sorry for her. Rose was very popular in Washington's social circles.

Insisting that Rose was a threat to the Union, Pinkerton suggested that she and her daughter be transferred to the Old Capitol Prison. Soon all of Washington buzzed with the news. On a day in January 1862, a crowd of curious people gathered outside her home. They dangled from trees and lampposts, craning their necks for a glimpse of the famous spy.

Rose strode defiantly down the steps of her home. When a reporter asked for her comments, she scoffed at Allan Pinkerton's detective abilities and complained that his "unwashed ruffians" had left footprints all over her fine rugs. Pinkerton saw to it that Rose was confined to a small, dingy cell in Old Capitol Prison.

Pinkerton and his men continued to round up spies and sympathizers. Meanwhile, Rose boldly made "tapestries," colorful balls of wool with secret messages tucked inside. She sewed a Confederate flag and waved it from her prison window.

Against Pinkerton's wishes, Lincoln exiled Rose Greenhow from the Union. In June 1862, she and her daughter were allowed to pass across enemy lines into Richmond, Virginia. There she wrote her memoirs and continued her Confederate activities.

Two years later, Rose tried to slip through a blockade of Union ships. When the boat she was traveling in overturned, Rose sank in the rough waters and drowned, her body weighted down with gold coins she had collected in Europe for the Confederacy.

Pinkerton had proved that Rose Greenhow was a spy, but he had never broken her will. In Greenhow, Allan Pinkerton had encountered a woman of iron, as determined a spy as he was a detective.

When President Lincoln visited McClellan's camp to review the troops, he would stop by Pinkerton's nearby tent and trade railroad stories with him. (Here, General John A. McClernand stands at right.)

On the Front Lines

1862-1865

While Allan Pinkerton was busy in Washington, agents Timothy Webster and Hattie Lawton were spying for the Union in Baltimore. Agent John Scully carried messages between Webster and Pinkerton.

Although Maryland had not seceded from the Union, Baltimore hummed with rebel activity. Pinkerton gave Webster a team of horses, a carriage, and enough money to visit the bars where Confederate sympathizers gathered. There, Webster openly criticized Lincoln and the Union. The tall, athletic Webster, at 40, was close to Pinkerton's age. Webster had a thatch of brown hair and deep-set gray eyes that could sparkle with mischief or flash in anger.

Before long Webster worked his way into a secret Confederate organization. He attended planning meetings and met with the group's leaders. Meanwhile, Pinkerton and his agents joined Union cavalry in a raid on the Confederate group the night Webster was scheduled to speak.

Close to midnight, Pinkerton and the soldiers surrounded the building. They watched as shadowy figures gave a rapping signal at the door, then entered. Timothy

Webster began to speak in a firm, convincing voice: "It will be our mission to strike directly at the heart of the Abolitionist party, and bury its foul carcass beneath the smoking ruins of Washington city!"

On cue, Pinkerton and his troops bashed in the door and stormed into the room. Webster ducked out the back door, following a preplanned escape route. The officers arrested the Confederate group's main plotters and took them to nearby Fort McHenry.

After this successful raid, Timothy Webster moved on to Richmond, Virginia, capital of the Confederacy. There he sent extremely detailed reports back to Pinkerton. Pinkerton considered Webster a genius and admired and valued his honesty, patriotism, and friendship.

After days of observation, the tireless Webster returned to Richmond. But early in February 1862, he became ill. In

Timothy Webster, Pinkerton's most famous spy

constant pain from acute rheumatism, a disease of the joints, all Webster could do was lie in his bed. Pinkerton sent agent Hattie Lawton to Richmond to care for Webster.

Webster was weak, exhausted, and had grown very thin. Agents Pryce Lewis and John Scully journeyed to Richmond to take over his spying activities. Unfortunately, while visiting Webster, Lewis and Scully were recognized by the son of a man they had once held under house arrest in Washington.

Shortly afterward, the two agents were arrested by Confederate authorities and jailed in Richmond. An escape attempt failed. Within a few weeks, they confessed to spying and told the Confederates of Webster's and Lawton's roles as spies.

Timothy Webster and Hattie Lawton were arrested by the Confederates in April 1862. Lawton, Lewis, and Scully received sentences of one to two years. Webster was sentenced to hang.

When Pinkerton heard the news, he was devastated. "My blood seemed to freeze in my veins—my heart stood still—I was speechless," he wrote later. He pleaded with President Lincoln to do something. The president sent a white flag delegation to Confederate President Jefferson Davis, asking him to spare Webster's life. Lincoln's carefully worded request carried an unspoken warning: Don't hang our spies, and we won't hang yours. President Davis refused.

Knowing he was doomed to die, a courageous and desperately ill Webster asked Hattie Lawton to tell Pinkerton, "I met my fate like a man. Thank him for his many acts of kindness to me. . . . I have done my duty and can meet death with a brave heart and a clear conscience."

A crowd of people watched in a carnival-like atmosphere. Armed soldiers ringed the gallows. The noose dangled. Crumpled on the floor was a black cap, ready to be dropped over Webster's head. The Confederates hanged Webster on April 29, 1862.

Through Pinkerton's efforts, Hattie Lawton was released soon after Webster's death. Lewis and Scully stayed in prison until 1863.

Pinkerton was now a trusted advisor to McClellan on the front lines. Pinkerton's scouts and spies helped carry messages and deliver orders. Allan's son William had left the University of Notre Dame to join his father. Willie wore old clothes and pretended to be a frightened country boy. He carried messages written on thin sheets of paper between his bare toes. If caught and questioned too closely, he could rub his feet together and lose the message in the dirt.

Pinkerton, now in his early 40s, must have been close to exhaustion during these long weeks and months. He gathered information at the front. At the same time, he dealt with

Willie spied for the Union army. He dressed in plain clothes or, as shown here at age 16, in a rebel uniform.

President Lincoln confers with General McClellan at Antietam.

complaints from the War Department. He also stayed in constant contact with George Bangs at the Chicago office. Whether noted on paper or stored in his amazing memory, Pinkerton rarely missed a detail.

Onc of Pinkerton's main jobs as chief intelligence officer was to estimate the numbers of Confederate troops. Pinkerton often overestimated these figures, and the inexperienced McClellan thought he was facing more troops than were actually there. Because of this misconception and his own natural caution, McClellan was slow to attack the enemy. Many in Washington criticized him; they said McClellan lacked courage.

McClellan first tried to capture Richmond, the Confederate capital, in April 1862. Pinkerton told McClellan that 180,000 troops defended the city. Actually, the Union forces greatly outnumbered the 85,000 Confederate troops.

Sometimes Pinkerton miscalculated because of his inexperience with wartime conditions. In his detective agency, he used carefully detailed reporting methods. Pinkerton's information now came from rebel deserters, refugees, and runaway slaves. Many of these people were terribly frightened and their reports were unreliable. Where 20 men with guns waited, Pinkerton's informers might report 40. A wagon train of 5 might be exaggerated to 15.

Pinkerton fiercely defended General McClellan against his Washington critics. Because of the embarrassment surrounding the Rose Greenhow spy case, Pinkerton suspected that he, too, was unpopular in Washington.

Pinkerton blamed McClellan's early military failures on President Lincoln's inexperience as commander-in-chief. It never crossed Pinkerton's mind that his own inaccurate numbers might have caused some of McClellan's errors in judgment.

McClellan battled Robert E. Lee's Confederate army at Antietam Creek, Maryland, in September 1862. In the intense heat of late summer, not a breath stirred the air. Suddenly, deafening sounds of shouts, screams, and gunfire exploded. As Pinkerton charged across the creek with the Union soldiers, the enemy opened fire, killing his beautiful reddish-brown horse. Unhurt, Pinkerton scrambled up behind another officer and escaped. When the fighting stopped, the

Crossing Antietam Creek, Pinkerton falls as his horse is killed underneath him.

ground was covered with thousands of soldiers' bodies, both Union and Confederate.

Pinkerton called Antietam a "brilliant and decisive victory" for McClellan and a "terrible blow to the South." Before the battle, McClellan and Pinkerton had believed Lee had 97,000 troops. In fact, McClellan's 70,000 troops greatly outnumbered Lee's 40,000 men. McClellan lost more than 12,000 soldiers in the battle, Lee more than 10,000. McClellan's failure to attack a second time allowed Lee's forces to escape. The day's combined death toll of nearly 23,000 men made Antietam one of the deadliest battles of all time.

President Lincoln questioned McClellan's actions when he met with Pinkerton in early October. Pinkerton strongly defended the general's moves. When he reported back to McClellan, Pinkerton downplayed Lincoln's concerns. For the next several weeks, McClellan and Lincoln communicated by telegram. Lincoln prodded the general to move against the enemy. The general asked for more men, supplies, and horses. Finally, President Lincoln removed McClellan as commander of the Army of the Potomac on November 7, 1862.

Furious, Pinkerton immediately resigned as head of the Secret Service. He returned to Chicago and threw his energies back into his own agency.

"No General . . . was ever so shamefully treated by his government, as was General McClellan," Pinkerton wrote later. With the same blind devotion he had shown toward radical abolitionist John Brown, Pinkerton saw only McClellan's strengths, not his weaknesses. Pinkerton even overlooked the fact that McClellan was opposed to freeing the slaves. The two remained lifelong friends.

On January 1, 1863, Lincoln issued the Emancipation Proclamation, freeing all slaves in the Confederate states. That same year, the Pinkerton's beloved daughter Belle, who had been sickly most of her life, died at the age of 20. Both Allan and Joan felt this loss deeply.

On April 9, 1865, the Civil War ended when Robert E. Lee surrendered to Ulysses S. Grant at Appomattox Court House, Virginia. The war had claimed a staggering number of human lives; 620,000 Union and Confederate soldiers had been killed. But the war had ended slavery as a way of life in the South.

Looking back proudly on his Civil War activities, Pinkerton wrote, "I rejoice in the freedom it brought to nearly half a million people . . . striking the shackles from their bruised limbs, and placing them before the law free and independent."

Five days after Appomattox, Pinkerton was in New Orleans chasing after cotton thieves when terrible news

President Lincoln is assassinated.

came. President Lincoln had been assassinated by John Wilkes Booth at Ford's Theatre in Washington. Pinkerton immediately sent word that he was available to help catch Lincoln's murderer.

Pinkerton felt that if he had been protecting the president that night at Ford's Theatre, no assassin could have come close to Lincoln. Back in 1861, during the long, eventful train ride to Lincoln's first inauguration, Pinkerton had warned Lincoln, "Sir, I beg of you, no matter what the circumstances, never attend the theatre."

In the last half of the 19th century, gangs of outlaws often traveled from place to place robbing banks, stagecoaches, and trains. Favorite targets were the trains carrying loads of currency and gold and silver coins.

The Renos' Reign of Terror

1866–1868

The money the Pinkerton Agency had earned during the war started it on another period of growth. Western Union hired Pinkerton to investigate wiretapping—illegal tapping on company telegraph lines. Railroads and express companies continued to turn to the Pinkertons as well.

To handle the increased business, the Pinkerton agency opened a New York office in 1866, headed by George Bangs. An office in Philadelphia opened the following year. Allan's two sons, William and Robert, had both joined the business. Each of them had inherited their father's leadership ability, strong business sense, and courage. William worked with his father in Chicago, supervising operations in the Midwest and West. Robert worked with George Bangs in New York.

Despite this expansion, Allan wanted to stay in complete control of the agency. He insisted on approving the investigation report on even the most minor case. This attention to detail meant long tiring days for Allan, now in his late 40s. The strain showed on his serious, dignified face.

A new kind of crime was on the rise. Gangs, often groups of brothers, banded together to rob neighborhood banks, county treasuries, stagecoaches, and trains. These "middle border bandits" thundered back and forth across the borders of Indiana, Illinois, Missouri, Iowa, and Minnesota. In many frontier towns, these gun-toting desperadoes were more powerful than the law.

Four of these bandits were the Reno brothers. Frank, John, and William Reno were in their 20s when they became outlaws; their brother Simeon was a teenager. From the fall of 1865 until the spring of 1866, the Renos and their gang terrorized the town of Seymour, Indiana, and the surrounding countryside, bursting into stores to empty cash registers. The gang also forced frightened citizens to pay bribes. Those who refused suffered torched barns, crippled cattle, and burned crops.

On a colorful fall day, October 6, 1866, the Reno gang robbed an Ohio & Mississippi Valley train. Wearing bandannas across their faces, John and Simeon Reno and

Frank Reno

Franklin Sparks jumped aboard the train as it puffed slowly out of Seymour. They quickly knocked the Adams Express guard unconscious.

Just outside of town, the bandits hurled two heavy safes containing $45,000 in gold and cash from the train. Other gang members waited to pick up the money.

The Adams Express company hired Allan Pinkerton to strike back at the Reno gang. A Seymour saloon keeper named Dick Winscott agreed to act as an informer for Pinkerton. Another Pinkerton plant pretended to be a railroad hand at the Seymour train depot. A gambling man in fancy clothes gathered information for Pinkerton as he flipped cards in the town saloon.

The saloon keeper made sure there were "fast" women and plenty of drinks to amuse the outlaws lounging around his smoky, dimly lit bar. One night, Winscott talked John Reno and Franklin Sparks into posing for a picture. The two men propped themselves up on a stool, waved their beer mugs, and smiled drunkenly at the camera. Their friends jeered and poked fun at Reno and Sparks.

After the Renos stole $22,065 from the Daviess County treasury in Gallatin, Missouri, Pinkerton decided the only way to stop the gang was to kidnap John Reno, their bright, crafty leader. Kidnapping was against the law, but Pinkerton felt strongly that breaking the law to catch a criminal was right.

Allan hired a special train from Cincinnati, Ohio, some 50 miles away. The sheriff of Daviess County met Allan at the Cincinnati station with a warrant for John Reno's arrest. Then Allan and six of his strongest men boarded the train bound for Seymour. Allan had sent instructions to the saloon keeper. Winscott's job was to get John Reno to walk down to the depot with him, supposedly to meet a friend.

This photograph, one of the few ever taken of John Reno (left), became part of Pinkerton's Rogue Gallery in Chicago.

The big black locomotive pulling Pinkerton's short train chugged toward Seymour. The gears moved slowly as the big iron wheels glided along ribbons of track. Plumes of steam from the wood-burning engine trailed behind the locomotive in the frosty air.

From the train window, Allan spotted Winscott standing on the platform, talking to a big man in a rumpled blue suit and crushed black hat. Allan studied the photograph Winscott had taken of John Reno. This was his man all right. The train's wheels were still in motion when Pinkerton and his agents jumped off.

Before a surprised John Reno knew what was happening, he was dragged, twisting and yelling, aboard the train. The train pulled out. Inside, the agents handcuffed Reno and tied him up. When news spread through Seymour that John Reno had been kidnapped, other gang members jumped on their horses. But they couldn't gallop fast enough to catch the train.

After spending the night in jail in Gallatin, Missouri, John Reno entered the penitentiary on January 18, 1868. Trials in frontier towns didn't always go according to the law. In a swift trial with no jury present, an angry judge slapped Reno into prison with a 20-year sentence.

Allan Pinkerton had thought kidnapping John Reno would throw the gang into confusion. He was wrong. Frank Reno took over as leader, and the gang continued its crime spree. The gang next stole $14,000 from the Harrison County treasury office in Magnolia, Iowa.

Allan put his son William, now 22, on the case. William and his men spent days traveling by buggy, questioning farmers in Council Bluffs, Iowa, about the gang. Then, when the time was right, the agents stormed the house where Frank Reno and four other gang members were hiding. Brandishing pistols, the agents broke down the door to find the outlaws eating breakfast. Frank Reno shouted and cursed at William. Behind the agents' backs, one of the outlaws slipped the Magnolia loot into a big potbellied stove. When William Pinkerton returned to the kitchen from a search of the house, he found $14,000 about to go up in smoke. He arrested the men and jailed them in Council Bluffs, Iowa.

On April 1, 1868, the day after the arrest, the agency's Chicago office received a telegram. The four prisoners had escaped. Over a hole they'd kicked in the wall, they had scrawled the words "APRIL FOOL."

A month later, the Renos committed their most famous robbery when they stole $96,000 in government bonds and gold from an Ohio & Mississippi Valley train in Marshfield near Seymour, Indiana. They beat the Adams Express messenger almost to death, then threw him off the train into a ditch. After this carefully planned robbery, the 12 gang members scattered to different locations.

The race was on. Who would capture the Renos? The Pinkertons or the growing numbers of citizens and railroad employees who were tired of living in terror? After combing the bushes of Coles County, Illinois, Allan and five agents rounded up three gang members in July 1868. But before Pinkerton could deliver his prisoners to the jail, an angry crowd took the law into its own hands. They seized the outlaws outside of Seymour and hanged them on the spot. The same month, a Pinkerton agent picked up William and Simeon Reno in Indiana.

Now Allan Pinkerton trailed Frank Reno and other gang members to Windsor, Canada, a rough border town across the river from Detroit, Michigan. Here, other American train robbers, safecrackers, and thugs congregated in saloons like the Windsor Turf Club, Manning's, and Rockford's, near the Windsor Ferry.

Allan and a posse of his agents finally arrested the last of the Reno gang. But Allan couldn't take his prisoners across the border yet. The Canadian and U.S. governments wrangled over international laws, forcing Allan to wait several months.

Meanwhile, several attempts were made on Allan's life. As he was walking down the ramp of the ferry in Detroit, he heard a pinging click right behind him. Allan whirled to find himself looking down the barrel of a gun. Quick as lightning, he jammed his finger into the trigger guard of the pistol and flipped the weapon out of the man's hand. Pinkerton wrestled his attacker to the ground, then marched the man straight to the Detroit police station.

At the station, Pinkerton learned the man was Dick Barry, a safecracker, who had been hired by a group of Windsor outlaws. A few days later, a second gunman unsuccessfully tried to kill Pinkerton. The gunman claimed to have been hired by the U.S. Secret Service. He later admitted that a rival private detective agency had hired him to "get the old Scotsman out of the way."

Finally, in late fall, Allan Pinkerton left Windsor with Reno. On the way to Detroit, the tugboat carrying Pinkerton and his four charges collided with a steamer and sank. Pinkerton and his agents frantically searched the icy waters of the Detroit River for their prisoners, who were weighted down by leg irons and handcuffs. The agents and their prisoners were finally dragged to safety aboard the steamer.

The group continued by steamboat, wagon, and buggy to New Albany, Indiana. There, an exhausted Pinkerton delivered the outlaws to the jail in which Simeon and William Reno were also being held.

As he handed over the prisoners, Pinkerton warned the sheriff that the jail was too flimsy to keep out a raging mob. He was right. On December 12, 1868, angry citizens stormed the jail. They hanged Frank, William, and Simeon Reno from the second-floor rafters of the rickety jail, along with Charlie Anderson, the gang's safecracker. The outlaws begged for mercy. But the citizens and other frightened prisoners watched the gang members die a slow, horrible death, twisting in agony at the end of a rope. At last, the Renos' reign of terror was over.

Larch trees form an archway over the road to the Pinkerton estate in Onarga, Illinois.

The Pressure Cooker Blows

1869–1871

No one suspected that, by 1869, Allan Pinkerton was a pressure cooker ready to blow. Now almost 50, he was a man driven by work. His Pinkerton's National Detective Agency was a million-dollar business, which included 20 detectives and 60 guards. Allan's stubborn attention to detail and need to be completely in charge began to exhaust his mind and body. Increasingly irritable, demanding, and unreasonable, he complained about mysterious "powers" threatening his agency.

The year before, Pinkerton agent Kate Warne had become seriously ill. Allan was at her bedside when she died at the age of 35. He had worked with her for 13 years; now he also missed her friendship. Some of his critics and even some members of his own family hinted he might have been in love with her. Kate Warne was buried in the Pinkerton family plot at Chicago's Graceland Cemetery. On her tombstone were the words, "Superintendent of the Female Detective Department of Pinkerton's National Police Agency."

In May 1868, Allan's older brother, Robert, also died. In spite of these tragedies, Allan refused to let his personal life affect his agency. He pushed forward, ignoring blinding headaches and other physical weaknesses.

In the late summer of 1869, Allan had a massive stroke, which in those days was called a "shock." His sons William and Robert told the public the stroke had been mild. They wanted people to still think of their father as a tough, powerful giant, the all-powerful "eye that never slept." In truth, the stroke had left Allan paralyzed, unable to speak or walk. He was totally dependent on his patient wife, Joan, and trusted friends and family. Doctors told him he'd never walk again. Allan fought that prognosis with all the strength he had left.

For a year, some of the best doctors in New York treated Allan. When that didn't help, he bathed in miracle springs. At home in Chicago, he forced himself into a routine of daily cold baths. Slowly, painful step by painful step, he did walk again, although one side of his body remained crippled. Gradually he learned to speak again. But it took the next few years for him to regain the ability to scrawl a shaky, childlike signature.

Robert and William now visited the branch offices, checked the ledgers, looked for new clients, and took charge of all agency investigations. During his recovery, Allan threw himself into building his family a summer home, a huge farm in Onarga, Illinois, 83 miles south of Chicago.

Allan named the estate The Larches, after the graceful arching trees that both he and Joan loved. Lining the winding driveways in rows and circling the house were 85,000 young larch trees he had ordered shipped from Scotland.

Surrounded by 12 acres of lawn, the white-pillared main house, called The Villa, had plenty of room for guests and a grand hall lit with crystal chandeliers for entertaining. On the wall were oil paintings of Civil War battles, views of the Scottish highlands, and portraits of famous people.

The 350 acres of elegant estate included a racetrack, fruit and vegetable gardens, greenhouses, a fish pond, 24 outbuildings, an icehouse, and a campground. For Joan, Allan had colorful beds of fragrant flowers planted everywhere. Thoroughbred horses, ponies, and cattle grazed in the pastures or fed in the big barns. Kennels on the estate echoed with the barking of dogs.

Years of fighting crime had made Pinkerton a cautious man. Armed guards watched each of the three entrances to the estate. At the top of The Villa, guards searched the grounds with binoculars for would-be attackers.

Leaning heavily on his cane, Allan walked the grounds of The Larches. When angry, he shook his walking stick and the thrum of his Scottish burr laced his halting speech.

The Villa, built in 1873. A cupola on the building's roof served as a lookout.

Allan and Joan spent many summer evenings walking through their flower gardens or along the many paths. On weekends, guests arrived in a special car on the Illinois Central train that ran through the property. A carriage with a uniformed driver met each train.

Besides his family, friends, and clients, many of America's most prominent people visited: Henry Sanford, president of the Adams Express Company; shipping and railroad tycoon "Commodore" Cornelius Vanderbilt; Ulysses S. Grant, then president of the United States; Chief Justice Salmon P. Chase; and Secretary of State William Seward. After dinner Joan took the women for a buggy ride. Allan and the men usually retired to The Snuggery—a long, low wine pavilion— to share Civil War stories. At times Allan could be a practical joker. A favorite stunt was to take his guests out fishing in his pond, then to upset the boat.

Onarga townsfolk were also welcome on the estate. They had to walk their horses though, so as not to scatter dust on Allan's roses. Sometimes neighborhood children came to ride the Shetland ponies.

When Allan returned to his Chicago office in the fall of 1871, everyone welcomed him back. He was slower but just as stubborn. But disaster followed Allan like a black cloud. In October 1871, a fire that started in a Chicago barn spread with the force of a hurricane. Soon the entire city, more than 2,000 acres, erupted into flames.

Pinkerton and his staff scurried to save what they could from the fierce wall of fire that jumped the river and roared up the streets. But within an hour, the Pinkerton office burned to the ground along with most of Chicago's business district.

The Chicago fire destroyed priceless early records at the Pinkerton agency, including the Rogues' Gallery and 400

Pinkerton headquarters was destroyed in the Great Chicago Fire, along with the rest of the city's downtown area.

volumes of criminal records. Allan also lost his treasured Secret Service files from the Civil War.

While buildings were still smoking, Allan hired carpenters to come in and start rebuilding. The fire had created new work for the agency. With only 310 police officers in Chicago, Pinkerton operatives were hired to guard many of Chicago's burned-out buildings from looters.

Pinkerton's National Detective Agency was rebuilt within the year. The new headquarters was a three-story building that housed offices for the guard service and the detective force. Tacked above the front door was the symbol of the all-seeing eye. Underneath were the words of the company motto, "We Never Sleep."

Jesse James was still a teenager when he started robbing banks and trains.

On the Trail of Jesse James

1871–1875

While Allan was rebuilding the agency, he crossed paths for the first time with outlaw Jesse James. Jesse led the James-Younger gang, which included Jesse's brother Frank, Cole Younger and his three brothers, and several other young men. Most of them had been guerrilla fighters for the Confederate captain William Quantrill during the Civil War. As "Quantrill Raiders," the men had been trained to kill or be killed.

The gang began their crime spree on February 3, 1866. On that day, they thundered into Liberty, Missouri, and robbed the Clay County Savings Association of $70,000, killing a young student.

Soon the James-Younger gang was robbing banks and trains all over the Midwest. When the bandits rode into town, their familiar war whoop sounded like an "evil gorilla yowl, a high-pitched yip, yip, aw, aw, aw." The haunting cry struck terror into the hearts of residents.

In 1871 a bank in Corydon, Iowa, hired Pinkerton's to stalk the gang. Pinkerton agents jumped on their horses and took off for Clay County, Missouri, where the James gang lived. There they found that local law officials were too scared to offer help. Too many relatives and friends of James gang members lived in the area.

When Pinkerton's first started trailing the James-Younger gang, no one even knew what Jesse James looked like. Jesse's mother wore the only picture of the Missouri outlaw in a heart-shaped locket around her neck. But slowly the agents began to gather details about the gang's leader. Of medium height, Jesse James had light blue eyes, heavy sandy whiskers, and broad shoulders. He had a slightly turned-up nose and a high forehead. People said Jesse talked like a well-educated man.

Pinkerton agents did not catch up with the gang on the first try. The gang's trail turned cold, as it would many times.

Meanwhile, the world and the nation were in the grips of a deep depression. Throughout the early 1870s, Allan Pinkerton struggled to save his agency. Once faithful railroad customers canceled contracts because they couldn't pay their bills. Allan's business fell $17,000 into debt.

Even though Pinkerton was frantic about keeping his agency afloat, he stayed strong for his sons. In a letter to William written November 7, 1872, Allan said, "I will come out all right, by'n bye . . . my idea is never to lose heart, never think for a moment of giving up the ship. I am bound to go through sink or swim."

Eventually, business picked up. In 1873, Allan and his agency helped crack a forgery ring that had swindled the Bank of England out of a million dollars. Then, in 1874, Pinkerton and his agency again took up the battle with Jesse James.

The James-Younger gang had continued to target banks and express companies. Pinkerton sent a large, raw-boned young agent, John W. Whicher, to Missouri. His job was to find work as a farmhand in Clay County and to try to win the confidence of the James gang.

In early March 1874, Whicher's mangled body was found dumped on the side of a road in Jackson County, Missouri. His hands had been tied behind his back. Bullets peppered his head, shoulders, and stomach. Part of Whicher's face had been chewed away by wild hogs. Everyone assumed the James gang was behind the murder.

Whicher's body lay in a cheap pine coffin at the Clay County mortuary. When Allan and his son William viewed the body, they were filled with white-hot rage. Soon after the murder, Pinkerton sent in Louis J. Lull, a former police captain, and two other men. Midafternoon on March 16, 1874, the three men were riding along Chalkhill Road when they heard hoofbeats behind them. Before they knew it, the Younger brothers, John and Jim, were upon them.

When the smoke cleared, John Younger was dead and agent Lull seriously wounded. Lull told his version of what had happened before he died at the nearby Roscoe Hotel.

In August 1874, Allan wrote an angry letter to George Bangs: "I know that the Jameses and the Youngers are desperate men, and that when we meet it must be the death of one or both of us . . . my [agents'] blood was spilt, and they [the gang] must repay. There is no use talking, they must die."

Several months later, Allan Pinkerton directed his agents to surround Castle James, the Missouri log cabin where the gang was supposed to be hiding out with Jesse and Frank's mother, Zerelda Samuels. Historians disagree about whether William Pinkerton participated in what happened next.

Near midnight on January 25, 1875, a slow-moving train crossed the Hannibal Bridge into Clay County, Missouri. The night was clear, with just a sliver of moon. The snow cast a pale, bluish sheen over the countryside. Only the steady click-clack of the iron-rimmed wheels sliced through the quiet.

A light still burned at Castle James. But word of the agents' arrival had spread. James gang members were already riding hard through the night toward a new location, from where they would fade into the remote hills.

The agents crept up to the cabin, with their "Greek fire-balls" ready. Pinkerton described these weapons as "balls of cotton well-saturated with combustible material." According to later reports, Pinkerton may have wanted so badly to catch the James gang that he used a real bomb.

Bashing in the boarded-up windows, the agents flung their fireballs into the cabin. The frightened occupants swept the fireballs into the fireplace filled with burning coals. The house lit up as it echoed with a woman's piercing scream. The explosion ripped off one arm of Zerelda, mother of the James boys, and killed their youngest half-brother, Archie, age eight. Blood spattered the walls.

When word of the raid hit the newspapers, local officials wanted the Pinkerton agents charged with murder. Lawmakers called for an investigation, but no action was taken. Allan Pinkerton defended his plan and his agents. He cited his murdered agents, Lull and Whicher. Castle James was probably the place where Whicher had been killed.

The raid on the Castle James hideout stirred up public sympathy for the gang. Many people already thought of Jesse James as a noble outlaw—a "cowboy Robin Hood." To them, his daring bandits robbed the railroads and banks that overcharged honest people. Forgotten were all the innocent

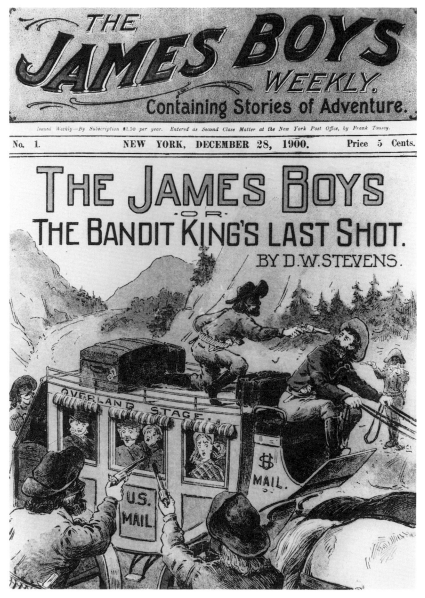

A boys' magazine from 1900 glamorized the exploits of Jesse and his gang. Jesse James had become legendary as a hero who robbed only the rich.

citizens these desperadoes had killed. In one robbery, the James gang had piled railroad ties onto a track so that a train carrying gold had toppled off the track. When the boiler overturned, the train's engineer was scalded to death and the stoker was badly burned.

Jesse James, with his little brother dead and his mother maimed, wanted revenge. He told his uncle, George Hite, "I could have killed the younger one [William Pinkerton] but I didn't. I wanted him to know who did it. . . . It wouldn't do me no good if I couldn't tell him about it before he died. I had a dozen chances to shoot him, but the opportunity never came. . . . I know God some day will deliver Allan Pinkerton into my hands."

Zerelda Samuels lost her right arm in the Pinkerton raid on the gang's hideout.

Railroads, frequent victims of the James gang, offered rewards for the gang's capture.

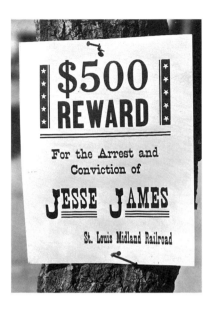

Jesse James never did get close enough to Allan Pinkerton to kill him. But the Pinkertons weren't the ones to bring down the gang, either. The remaining Younger brothers were arrested in Northfield, Minnesota, and served time in the Minnesota State Prison in Stillwater. Jesse James was eventually shot and killed, for money, by a fellow gang member, Robert Ford. The banks, express companies, and railroads that the James-Younger gang had robbed probably paid the reward.

Jesse James and his gang eluded Allan Pinkerton. But during the heyday of gang robberies, Pinkerton and his agents brought many other outlaws to justice.

The Molly Maguires were a secret society of laborers who banded together during Ireland's potato famine, from 1846 to 1852. When Mollies immigrated to the United States in the 1860s, many of them settled in Pennsylvania's coalfields, where they continued to meet in secret.

The Molly Maguires

1873-1877

After years of protecting big businesses and industries from lawlessness, Allan held different views than he'd held as a young Chartist in Scotland. In 1873, Allan accepted a job that pitted his agency against the growing labor movement in the United States. His agents now faced off opposite the type of poor, mistreated worker that Allan himself had once been.

Workers in many industries had begun to fight for better wages, conditions, and hours, and they had banded together into labor unions. Coal miners' unions protested the often unbearable conditions that miners suffered. Coal miners worked 14 hours a day in narrow underground tunnels, where the coal dust was so thick that workers could barely breathe. Often soaked to the skin by seeping groundwater, the miners pounded the hard coal out of the earth with picks and axes. Injuries and deaths from explosions and poison gases were frequent. The deadly disease called black lung, caused by coal dust, slowly and painfully strangled the miners' lungs.

At the end of a long, backbreaking month, miners received a slip of paper called "scrip." This "money" could only be used at company-owned stores, where goods were over-priced. After miners paid for rent, food, and equipment, little was left of their monthly wages.

Many early labor unions sincerely wanted to make things better for miners. But some groups were suspected of using violent and devious tactics to fight the coal bosses. Back in the 1860s in eastern Pennsylvania's Schuylkill County, 50 people had been stabbed, shot, beaten, and muti-lated. In many cases, bodies of victims disappeared. Other violent acts followed—railcar derailments, buildings set on fire, and threats against mine superintendents.

At that time, people considered newly arrived Irish im-migrants dangerous. Anti-Catholic sentiment was also com-mon. The Molly Maguires were immigrant coal miners who

A coal industry executive is shot.

Agent James McParland

belonged to a secret society in eastern Pennsylvania. Because they were both Irish and Catholic, it was easy to blame the lawless conditions on the Mollies.

Franklin Gowen, president of the Philadelphia and Reading Railroad and the Coal and Iron Company, wanted Pinkerton's agency to crack the legendary Molly Maguire gang. Pinkerton decided that the right agent for the Molly job was James McParland, who had joined the agency the year before.

Allan knew that 29-year-old McParland had a sound, logical mind and a good memory. He might be strong enough to take on this dangerous assignment. McParland also had worked as a teamster, meat wagon driver, deckhand, bartender, and private police officer. This varied background and his strong Irish accent might help him win acceptance from the Mollies without suspicion.

McParland takes the oath of the Molly Maguires.

McParland's job was to break into the inner circle of the Mollies and report all movements of the gang to the Philadelphia office. Allan wanted names of members, a list of crimes committed, and code words. He would pay McParland $12 each week, whether he succeeded or failed.

Over the next several days, Allan gave the young man detailed instructions. Then, neatly dressed James McParland became bedraggled-looking James McKenna, supposedly fleeing a murder charge. He boarded a train bound for Philadelphia on October 27, 1873.

Pinkerton joked that even McParland's own mother wouldn't have recognized him. Formerly clean shaven except for a moustache, he now had a beard. His usually well-groomed, reddish-brown hair was scraggly and unkempt. McParland's worn clothing included a dirt-colored slouch hat, a coarse gray coat, oversized pants of brown wool tied with a leather belt, and a pair of hobnailed, high-top boots. A ragged carpetbag contained a change of clothes, stamps, envelopes, and writing paper.

Once in the eastern Pennsylvania coal fields, McParland, posing as McKenna, traveled from town to town. He'd sing, dance a jig, and talk with the coal miners in the bars. But behind the rowdiness and idle conversation, McParland found out all he could about the Mollies.

At the Sheridan House in Pottsville, McParland boasted, brawled, and drank with mine workers who were supposed to be part of the Mollies' inner circle. Many carried guns or billy clubs and wore steel knuckles. Soon, McParland rented a room above the barroom of "Muff" Lawler, a gigantic man who was leader of the Mollies in Shenandoah, 20 miles away.

Late at night, McParland wrote his secret reports to Pinkerton. At first he wrote with ink made from chimney soot and water. Later, Lawler gave him bluing, a liquid used to wash clothes, to use for ink. With stamps he kept in his shoe, McParland then would sneak out alone in the darkness to mail the letters at post offices in nearby towns. Pinkerton's Philadelphia superintendent sent coded messages back with instructions.

On April 13, 1874, McParland was initiated into the Ancient Order of Hibernians, a secret group to which all the Mollies belonged. He paid the $3 fee and took an oath of "friendship, unity, and Christian charity." Then he solemnly repeated the Molly signs and passwords.

As McParland became more and more a part of the complex web of the Mollies, he continued to send secret messages back to Allan Pinkerton. Because McParland could read and write (most Mollies could not), the Mollies made him secretary of the group. Over the next three years, the Molly Maguire file at Pinkerton's grew. Frustrated with the length of the investigation, Pinkerton called the Mollies a "species of thugs."

In September 1874, McParland met briefly with Pinkerton in Philadelphia. Allan was shocked by the state of McParland's health. Long hours spent coal mining, bad food and whiskey, and the pressures of living a spy's life had made McParland look gaunt and worn.

Conditions in the mines grew worse. In the Long Strike from Christmas 1875 to the following June, workers angry about pay cuts closed down the mines. To protect strike-breakers, the Coal and Iron Company hired 18 Pinkerton agents to act as police, led by undercover Pinkerton agent Robert Linden.

Meanwhile, the violence in the mining towns continued. People suspected of sympathizing with the mine owners were murdered, their homes torched. Railroad owners accused workers of dumping coal cars, burning toolhouses, and de-stroying tracks.

Early in 1876, the Molly grapevine buzzed with rumors. Someone had posted a secret membership list. People spec-ulated that the person who had done it could read and write and must be an insider. Molly leaders grew suspicious. Then a train conductor recognized McParland as a Pinkerton de-tective. The conductor told a key Molly.

McParland sensed his life was in grave danger. On March 7, 1876, he contacted agent Robert Linden. The two made a hasty escape by train to Philadelphia, and James McKenna vanished forever.

McParland's testimony in a Pottsville courtroom later helped convict and hang 19 gang members in June 1877.

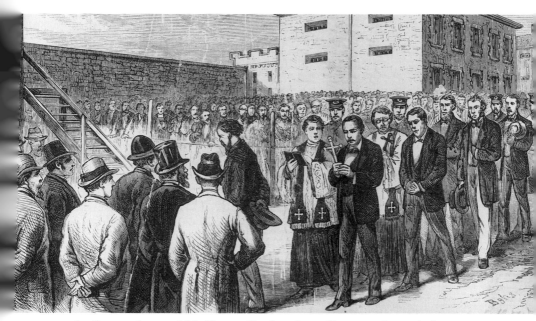

As the condemned Mollies walked to the gallows, each carried a crucifix and wore a rose.

People then argued about whether Allan Pinkerton and his agents had done something good or bad by crushing the Mollies. Increasingly Pinkerton and his agency were seen as enemies of labor, tools of the "robber barons" who made the workers' lives miserable. Other people praised the Pinkertons, calling the cracking of the Molly Maguires a triumph for the public good.

After the hangings, the Mollies disbanded. The truth about this group may never be known. The Molly Maguires may have been blamed for crimes that other groups committed, and the Mollies who died may have been innocent. For more than 100 years, the Molly Maguire debate has raged in courtrooms, living rooms, and history books. With each retelling of the story, more facts have twisted into legend.

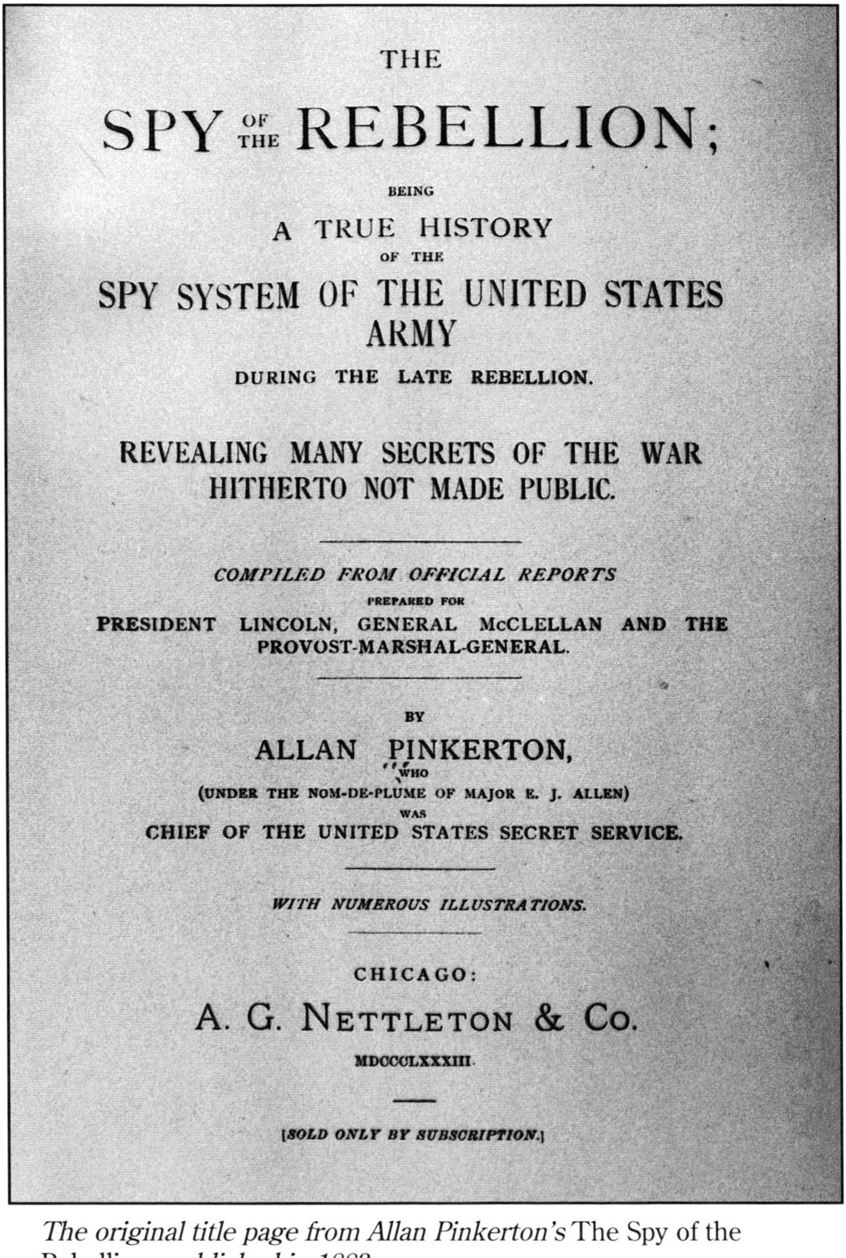

THE

SPY OF THE REBELLION;

BEING

A TRUE HISTORY

OF THE

SPY SYSTEM OF THE UNITED STATES
ARMY

DURING THE LATE REBELLION.

REVEALING MANY SECRETS OF THE WAR
HITHERTO NOT MADE PUBLIC.

COMPILED FROM OFFICIAL REPORTS
PREPARED FOR
PRESIDENT LINCOLN, GENERAL McCLELLAN AND THE
PROVOST-MARSHAL-GENERAL.

BY

ALLAN PINKERTON,
"WHO
(UNDER THE NOM-DE-PLUME OF MAJOR E. J. ALLEN)
WAS
CHIEF OF THE UNITED STATES SECRET SERVICE.

WITH NUMEROUS ILLUSTRATIONS.

CHICAGO:

A. G. NETTLETON & CO.

MDCCCLXXXIII.

[SOLD ONLY BY SUBSCRIPTION.]

The original title page from Allan Pinkerton's The Spy of the
Rebellion, *published in 1883*

Last Days

1875–1884

The Molly Maguires case was the last one Allan directly supervised. People often spotted him on city streets, however, a gray-haired, bearded man leaning heavily on the arm of one of his sons. Though his mind remained sharp, Allan's stroke had left him crippled and fragile. He fought to improve his slurred speech, but his words often came out garbled. Glasses perched on the end of his nose.

Partially retired, Allan turned to writing detective novels. Americans at that time loved melodramatic mystery stories, which were published in cheap "dime novels." His first book, *The Expressman and the Detective,* covered the 1858 Maroney robbery. Published in 1875, when Allan was 56, the book sold 15,000 copies within two months.

Publishers encouraged Allan to write more. *The Spy of the Rebellion* told the "true history" of the Civil War spy system and the adventures of Timothy Webster. Besides these popular books, Allan wrote *The Molly Maguires and the Detectives* and 15 others.

Allan always made his main characters look strong and honorable. The books all had the same theme—detectives were needed and worthy of respect. But sometimes Allan made the detective look so clever and cunning that readers rooted for the criminal.

A tremor in Allan's hands made writing by hand nearly impossible, so he dictated the outlines for his books. Professional writers then helped him polish and perfect the stories. Drawing on his enormous memory, he'd add details—the curl of a moustache, the sound of a voice, an unexpected challenge, a clever disguise.

Supervision of the major cases had now passed into the hands of William and Robert. Yet Allan remained keenly interested in the agency he had founded. Each morning a handsome horse-drawn carriage called a barouche took him to the Chicago office. There he read stacks of reports on cases and dictated letters. He offered advice, praise, and some orders.

Robert Pinkerton   *William Pinkerton*

Allan continued to push for women in the agency over the objections of his sons and George Bangs. When agents in the Philadelphia office wanted Sundays off to attend church, he ordered the agents to be at the office by 9:00 on Sunday mornings. Allan wanted his sons, George Bangs, and others to know that it was still his agency; he was still the boss.

Trouble was also simmering at home. Allan still thought of his pretty, vivacious daughter Joan as his little girl. When he was away from home, he sent her letters decorated with his tiny sketches of kittens. In 1876, Joan, then 21, fell in love with a young businessman, William J. Chalmers.

When Joan asked permission to marry Chalmers, Pinkerton flatly refused. Allan complained to Robert that he didn't think Chalmers had the necessary brain power and would make a poor husband for Joan.

One night Allan stumbled across his daughter and Chalmers kissing good night in the parlor with the lights turned low. Furious, Pinkerton banished Chalmers from the house. Soon after this incident, Joan kissed her mother a tearful good-bye, left her parents' house, and headed for New York to live with her brother Robert.

Allan also worried about his wife. Joan was ill with heart problems and had to stay in bed most of the time. On their 35th anniversary in March 1877, he dictated a tender letter to "My Dear Little Wife" in which he spoke fondly about all they had shared together in their marriage:

> I know, since you were eighteen years of age you have been battling with me, side by side, willing to do anything to bear our children and work hard, yet you never found fault. . . . Let us wish we may be spared a few more years . . . enjoying happiness and health to ourselves, our children, and our friends.

Eventually, daughter Joan returned home. It was obvious that Allan's anger had more to do with his daughter challenging his rules than with her wanting to get married. She married William Chalmers in a stylish wedding attended by all the Pinkertons and most of Chicago's wealthy families.

Allan found it difficult to admit that his sons had their own strengths, responsibilities, and families, too. He thought jovial, outgoing William drank to excess and spent too much money. Like his father, William had a fiery temper and was good at managing the detective force and tracking criminals. But because they both worked in the Chicago office, his father kept a close watch on everything William did.

Robert had inherited his father's high energy and his mother's patience. But, in 1879, he announced that he wanted a share of the growing profits of Pinkerton's, rather than a salary. He threatened to quit the agency and change his name. Insulted and hurt, Allan threatened to immediately replace Robert in the agency.

Gradually the stormy waters calmed, both in the family and at the agency. Beneath Allan Pinkerton's bluster and unreasonable demands lay a deep sadness. Allan knew that his steamrolling energy and quick mind were trapped inside a failing body.

As the tremors in Allan's hands and speech worsened, he began to spend more time sitting in his garden or by the fireside, which he loved. Joan, now in her late 50s, sometimes joined him. But rheumatism made her bones and muscles ache, so she spent many hours confined to her bed. Before she had grown frail, Allan and Joan had made several trips back to Scotland to visit friends and family. But now the two stayed close to home. Daughter Joan, now a mother herself, often brought their grandchildren to visit.

One day in 1881, Allan's son William brought sad news to the house. A telegram had arrived at the office announcing that George Bangs had died. On hearing of the death of his friend of 30 years, Allan clutched his cane with both hands. Tears rolled down his cheeks.

By the spring of 1884, the family sensed that Allan was dying. He was weak, yet he still insisted on pushing himself to walk, if only a few steps. In a bad fall in June, he bit his tongue and was knocked unconscious. The tongue became infected; Allan never regained consciousness. On July 1, 1884, at the age of 64, Allan Pinkerton died with his family at his side.

At the news of his death, newspapers carried glowing articles about him. One account began, "Few lives have been as crowded with exciting incidents as Allan Pinkerton's." Another called him bold, shrewd, loyal, iron willed, and skillful. Writers credited him with having given dignity to the detective profession. With his unhesitating courage and strong business skills, he had founded an organization known and respected all over the world.

Allan Pinkerton was buried at Chicago's Graceland Cemetery. He left an estate worth half a million dollars. In his will, Allan had left his property—including his beloved Larches farm and another farm called The Catalpas—to his wife, his books and copyrights to his daughter Joan, and the agency to his sons.

Without Allan, the elder Joan—Allan's "wee bonnie lass"—seemed to lose her will to live. On January 22, 1887, Joan died at the age of 65. Just before she died, Joan whispered to William that she was going to join his father.

The Pinkerton agency's New York City office in the early 1900s

The Agency Today

After Allan's death, William continued his father's detective work in the western division of the agency. At the turn of the century, William became an expert on the shadowy figures of the underworld—the Mafia. Like his father, he earned the nickname "The Eye."

Robert became the head of the New York office after George Bangs's death. With his talent for administration and business, he expanded the agency by enlarging the guard service and opening offices in 10 other cities.

As the agency grew, people began to refer to it as America's Scotland Yard. William and Robert and their agents chased after such notorious criminals as Adam Worth, Butch Cassidy and the Sundance Kid, and other stagecoach, bank, and train robbers in the American West and elsewhere. After William and Robert died, Robert's son, Allan, Jr., and his grandson, Robert A. Pinkerton, carried on the business, adding up to four generations of Pinkerton detectives.

Not everyone thought highly of the work done by Pinkerton's in the late 1890s and early 1900s. Labor leaders thought that spying on employees violated workers' rights.

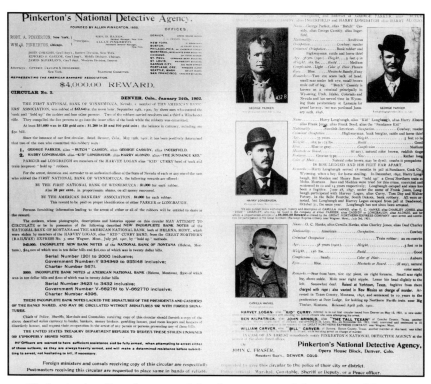

Pinkerton's offered a reward for the capture of the train robbers known as the Wild Bunch, who included Butch Cassidy and the Sundance Kid.

Pinkerton agents who protected railroad officials against striking workers were called vipers, scoundrels, spies, bandits, and a threat to freedom. One of the ugliest clashes took place in 1892, during the Homestead Strike between Carnegie Steel Company and steelworkers in Homestead, Pennsylvania. When gunfire broke out between 376 Pinkerton guards hired by Carnegie and striking steelworkers, 3 guards and 10 workers were killed.

Encino, California, is now the site of the corporate headquarters of Pinkerton Security and Investigation Services. A massive Diebold safe with a combination lock stands in the lobby. The black cast-iron safe on four legs comes from a time when there were no armored trucks, no huge bank vaults, no safe places to keep money—a time when the first Pinkerton operatives chased railroad and express company bandits by train, horseback, or on foot.

No Pinkerton family members are part of the modern agency. But reminders of the Pinkerton dynasty are everywhere. Pictures of Allan and his sons hang on the wall. Display cases hold copies of all the books Allan Pinkerton wrote, his big gold watch engraved with the intertwined initials "AP," pictures of his Chicago office, and century-old pistols. A worn black leather book contains secret code names for former Pinkerton agents. All the aliases end in "wood"—Robert A. Pinkerton was "Lowood," other agents were "Conkwood" and "Flapwood." A picture of Timothy Webster hangs on the wall, along with samplings from the Rogues' Gallery.

Many things have changed in the modern agency. The company motto is no longer "We Never Sleep," but "The Best People for the Job." Operatives are now called security officers. The company logo is a streamlined version of the original eye. In addition to some of Allan Pinkerton's pioneering methods, today's agents use computerized data banks, zoom lenses, listening devices, night vision enhancers, car phones, binoculars, and other electronic devices.

Pinkerton Security and Investigation Services is one of the world's largest private investigation services. It employs 45,000 people in 200 offices in the United States, Canada, Mexico, and the United Kingdom. The wealthiest companies in the United States are among its 9,000 clients.

Pinkerton agents have provided protection during several Olympics and world's fairs. Pinkerton officers protect movie stars, business executives, presidents, heads of state, and diplomats. Agency detectives still guard property and investigate wrongdoing inside big companies. But some of the work done by the early Pinkerton agency is now handled by police forces, the Secret Service, and the F.B.I.

The Pinkertons made history. Their story began with a maverick Scotsman who founded the first detective bureau in the United States and helped shape the meaning of the word "detective" for decades to come.

At Pinkerton corporate headquarters, tall filing cabinets hold hundreds of letters, records, and pictures. The yellowed paper falls apart at the touch of a hand, but their words bring to life one of the most colorful men of the 19th century.

Sources

p.8 Allan Pinkerton, *The Spy of the Rebellion,* (Chicago: A. G. Nettleton, 1883), 201.

p.12 G. C. Symons, "My Visit to the Wynds of Glasgow: Reports from Assistant Hand-loom Weaver Commissioners," 1839, 51.

p.19 Edgar L. Wakeman, "Allan Pinkerton: Reminiscences of the Early Life of a Great Detective," *Evening Star* (Philadelphia), 21 September 1889.

p.20 Ibid.

p.20 Ibid.

p.21 Ibid.

p.21 Letter, 6 October 1861, Pinkerton Papers, Library of Congress.

p.25 Edgar L. Wakeman, "Allan Pinkerton: Reminiscences of the Early Life of a Great Detective."

p.25 Ibid.

p.25 Ibid.

p.26 Ibid.

p.30 Allan Pinkerton, *Professional Thieves and the Detective,* 24.

p.30 Ibid.

p.32 Ibid., 33–34.

p.33 Ibid., 54.

p.39 Allan Pinkerton, *General Principles of Pinkerton's National Detective Agency* (Chicago: Fergus Printing, 1873), 6.

p.41 *Daily Democratic Press* (Chicago), 9 September 1853.

p.43 Papers, Pinkerton Security & Investigation Services.

p.46 James D. Horan, *The Pinkertons: The Detective Dynasty that Made History,* (New York: Crown, 1967), 38.

p.47 Lloyd Lewis, "Lincoln and Pinkerton," *Journal of the Illinois State Historical Society,* Volume XLI, No. 4, December 1948, 376.

p.48 Allan Pinkerton, *Expressman and the Detective* (New York: W. B. Keen, Cooke & Co., 1873), 95.

p.49 James D. Horan, *The Pinkertons: The Detective Dynasty that Made History,* 45.

p.49 Frank Morn, *The Eye that Never Sleeps* (Bloomington, Indiana: Indiana University Press, 1982), 23.

p.49 *Daily Democratic Press* (Chicago), 17 March 1855.

p.54 Frank Morn, *The Eye that Never Sleeps,* 60.

p.54 "The Baltimore Plot to Assassinate Abraham Lincoln," *Harper's New Monthly* Magazine, June 1868.

p.55 Norma Cuthbert, ed., *Lincoln and the Baltimore Plot,* 1861 (San Marino, California: Huntington Library, 1949), 110.

p.58 Cuthbert, *Lincoln & the Baltimore Plot,* 84.

p.59 Allan Pinkerton, *Spy of the Rebellion,* 103.

p.67 Ishbel Ross, *Rebel Rose,* (New York: Harper & Brothers, 1954), 142.

p.72 Allan Pinkerton, *The Spy of the Rebellion,* 298.

p.73 Ibid., 544.

p.73 Ibid., 554.

p.77 Ibid., 571

p.78 Ibid.

p.78 Ibid., 585.

p.79 Archie McFeidres, "When Pinkerton Saved Lincoln's Life," *Coronet Magazine,* February 1944.

p.87 Frank Morn, *The Eye that Never Sleeps,* 74.

p.95 Allan Hynd, "On the Outlaw Trail with the Pinkertons," *Master Detective Magazine,* 1 October 1945.

p.96 Letter, 7 November 1872, Pinkerton Papers, Library of Congress.

p.97 Letter, 17 August 1874, Pinkerton Papers, Library of Congress.

p.98 Letter, 27 January 1875, Pinkerton Archives.

p.100 James D. Horan, *The Pinkertons: The Detective Dynasty that Made History,* 202.

p.107 Allan Pinkerton, *The Molly Maguires and the Detectives,* (New York: Dover Publications) 1873, 17.

p.108 Letter, 29 August 1875, Pinkerton Papers, Library of Congress.

p.113 Letter 28 March 1877, Pinkerton Papers, Library of Congress.

p.115 *Harper's Weekly* (New York), 12 July 1884.

Bibliography

"Allan Pinkerton, Detective," *Harper's Weekly*, 12 July 1884.

"Allan Pinkerton Pioneered on the Illinois Central," *Illinois Central Magazine*, January 1946.

Annan, Thomas. *Old Closes and Streets of Glasgow 1868/1877.* New York: Dover, 1977.

"The Baltimore Plot to Assassinate Abraham Lincoln," *Harper's New Monthly Magazine*, June 1868.

Chalmers, Joan Pinkerton. "When the Pinkertons Came to Chicago," *Chicago Daily News*, 27 May 1931.

Coleman, J. Walter. *The Molly Maguire Riots.* Richmond, Virginia: Richmond-Garrett and Massie, 1936.

Cuthbert, Norma, ed. *Lincoln and the Baltimore Plot, 1861.* San Marino, California: Huntington Library, 1949.

DeWees, F. P. *The Molly Maguires.* New York: Burt Franklin, 1877.

Fowler, Professor O. S. *Phrenological Description of Allan Pinkerton,* Esq. Chicago: Lakeside Publishing and Printing Company, 1874.

Glasser, Ralph. *Growing Up in the Gorbals.* London: Pan Books, 1986.

Herndon, William H. and Jesse W. Weik. *Herndon's Life of Lincoln.* Edited by Paul M. Angle. Greenwich, Connecticut: Fawcett Publications, undated.

Hertz, Emanuel. *The Hidden Lincoln.* New York: Viking Press, 1938.

Horan, James D. *Desperate Men.* New York: G. P. Putnam's Sons, 1949.

_____. *Desperate Women.* New York: G. P. Putnam's Sons, 1952.

_____. *The Pinkertons: The Detective Dynasty that Made History.* New York: Crown, 1967.

Horan, James D., and Howard Swiggart. *The Pinkerton Story.* New York: G. P. Putnam's Sons, 1951.

Hynd, Allan. "On the Outlaw Trail with the Pinkertons," *Master Detective Magazine*, 1 October 1945.

Kelley, William D. *Lincoln and Stanton.* New York: G. P. Putnam's Sons, 1885.

Lewis, Lloyd. "Lincoln and Pinkerton," *Journal of the Illinois State Historical Society*, Volume XLI, No. 4, December 1948.

Lossing, Benson J. *Mathew Brady's Illustrated History of the Civil War.* New York: Fairfax Press, undated.

Marcy, General R. B. "Detective Pinkerton," *Harper's Monthly*, October 1873.

McFeidres, Archie. "When Pinkerton Saved Lincoln's Life," *Coronet Magazine*, February 1944.

Morn, Frank. *The Eye That Never Sleeps.* Bloomington, Indiana: Indiana University Press, 1982.

Papers. Pinkerton Security & Investigation Services, Encino, California.

Ross, Ishbel. *Rebel Rose.* New York: Harper & Brothers, 1954.

Rowan, Richard. "Secret Police: Case No. 1—The First Plot Against Lincoln," *American Police Review,* September-October 1937.

"The Scotch in Chicago," *Scottish American Journal,* 16 September 1875.

Sears, Stephen W., ed. *The Civil War Papers of George B. McClellan.* New York: Ticknor & Fields, 1989.

Wakeman, Edgar L. "Allan Pinkerton: Reminiscences of the Early Life of a Great Detective," *Evening Star* (Philadelphia), 21 September 1889.

Writings of Allan Pinkerton

Expressman and the Detective. Chicago: W. B. Keen, Cooke & Co., 1875.

General Principles of Pinkerton's National Detective Agency, Chicago: Fergus Printing, 1873.

"History and Evidence of the Passage of Abraham Lincoln from Harrisburg, Pennsylvania, to Washington, February 22 and 23, 1861." Chicago: no publisher named, 1868.

The Molly Maguires and the Detectives. New York: Dover Publications, 1877.

Strikers, Communists, Tramps, and Detectives. New York: G. W. Carleton, 1878.

Professional Thieves and the Detective. New York: G. W. Carleton, 1880.

The Spy of the Rebellion. Chicago: A. G. Nettleton, 1883.

Letter to William H. Herndon, 23 August 1866, Chicago Historical Society.

Letters. Huntington Library, San Marino, California.

Letters. Pinkerton Security & Investigation Services, Encino, California.

Index

Illustration Acknowledgments

The photographs and illustrations in this text have been reproduced through the courtesy of:
pp. 1, 22, 34, 91, The Chicago Historical Society; pp. 2, 6, 80, 93, 99, 101, 104, 109, 118, The Bettman Archive; pp. 9, 14, 31, 33, 39, 40, 44, 54, 56, 58, 64, 66, 74, 77, 82, 84, 100, 105, 106, 110, 112, (both), 116, Pinkerton's Security & Investigation Services; pp. 10, 12, 19, The Mansell Collection; p. 16 by Darren Erickson; pp. 24, 91, New York Historical Society; p. 26, Dundee Township Historical Society; p. 29, Archive Photos; pp. 37, 46, 75, 79, 94, 102, Library of Congress; pp. 42, 68, 70, National Archives; p. 50, Library of Virginia; p. 52, U.S. Army; pp. 62, 72, Lieb Image Archives; p. 88, New York Public Library.

Front cover illustration and photograph courtesy Archive Photos. Back cover illustration reprinted from *The Spy of the Rebellion* by Allan Pinkerton.

page 2: *Allan Pinkerton on horseback at Antietam, Maryland. Pinkerton served as Secret Service chief for the Union's Army of the Potomac.*
page 6: *Pinkerton, seated at right, with a group of his Secret Service agents*